THE EDGARS FOREVER

PUBLISHED IN ASSOCIATION WITH
EVEREST DOUBLE GLAZING

THE EDGARS FOREVER

ANN MARTIN

PELHAM BOOKS
LONDON

First published in Great Britain by
PELHAM BOOKS LTD
44 Bedford Square
London WC1B 3DU
1984

Cataloguing in publication data

Martin, Ann
   The Edgars forever.
   1. Show jumpers (Persons) – Biography
   I. Title
   798.2′5′0922   SF295.2
ISBN 0 7207 1504 0

Printed in Great Britain by
Butler & Tanner Ltd, Frome and London

FRONTISPIECE: Forever, Nick, Liz and Ted at home. (*Bob Langrish*)

*To my husband
Francis*

CONTENTS

Abbreviations Used in the Text

AIT   Area International Trial

BSJA   British Show Jumping Association

CSIO   Concours Sauté Internationale Officiale

FEI   Fédération Equestre Internationale

MFH   Master of Foxhounds

PREFACE

Over a quarter of a century ago, Colonel Sir Harry Llewellyn, later to be Chairman of the Selection Committee, had the foresight to write about Ted's international debut in Rotterdam: 'Ted jumped two clear rounds with his plucky and extremely obedient mare Jane Summers and proved himself to have a splendid match temperament. He is a valuable potential in terms of Olympic Games.'

For a variety of reasons, an Olympiad appearance was not to be. But these early experiences, coupled with the sage advice he gained from his marriage to Liz Broome, were contributory to the establishment of the Everest Stud as one of the world's most powerful by 1980.

Liz keeps a plaque with the following prayer on the wall above her desk: 'God grant me the serenity to accept the things I cannot change: courage to change those things I can and wisdom to know the difference.' (By the Rev. Doctor Reinhold Niebuhr, Massachusetts.) She has inherited immeasurable strength of character from her Welsh–Scots forbears and these words represent her concept of life.

To write *The Edgars Forever* was a challenging prospect and I would like to thank Liz for her friendship, kindness and guidance through the web of people and events that have led to the formation of the stud as it is today. Also David and Jane Kingsley, without whose help the book would not have been possible.

Others I wish to thank are Gina Hayes, who deciphered my illegible handwriting into immaculate script, and the wonderful back-up team who tended my house, horses and garden so well while I wrote the book.

Not least my husband Francis for his patience, understanding and sense of humour.

THE EVEREST CONNECTION

From an early age, Mr David Kingsley, one of four partners who started Everest Double Glazing in 1965, had been interested in horses. This enthusiasm, which started during his childhood in India where his father kept a racing stable, did not diminish throughout his rise in the world of British business.

Everest had been in business for three years when two things happened which were to play a major part in the company's future tie-up with show-jumping. An enterprising Everest District Manager decided, off his own bat, to sponsor a small event at his local county show, the South of England at Ardingly in Sussex. Almost at the same time, David Kingsley was introduced to Robert Dean, the man who was the power behind most successful sponsorship link-ups in the equestrian world. It was Dean, later to become chairman of British Equestrian Promotions, who suggested Everest should 'wet its feet' by running a meeting designed to give riders indoor practice before the important annual Horse of the Year Show which heralds the winter circuit. This three-day show at Park Farm has, over the years, become a major event in its own right.

It was through Dean that Kingsley met Ted Edgar, already a well-known rider who was looking for support. He had just won the 1969 King George V Gold Cup on Uncle Max and also owned the promising Snaffles. This meeting led to Kingsley's company leasing the two horses on a trial run. Uncle Max was soon to retire, but Snaffles went on to win a number of important championships, including the company's own, then held at the British Equestrian Centre, Stoneleigh.

Soon after, David Kingsley realised his wish to become more involved. With his wife Jane, Ted Edgar and his wife Liz, he set up the Everest Stud. The Stud's long-term aim was to buy and bring on show-jumpers. Everest Double Glazing would continue to have the pick of the show-jumpers to lease, but the stable would remain free to have other owners in the yard.

The partnership, which started over a decade ago in 1973, was to mature, expand and flourish. Horses bought by the Stud along the way included Boomerang who was first produced by Liz. Boomerang went on to become one of the most successful and famous show-jumpers of all time with a record four consecutive victories to his credit in the notoriously difficult Hickstead Derby with his final rider Eddie Macken.

Today, the Everest Stud maintains a strength of about twenty horses including such well-known names as Everest Forever, Everest If Ever, Everest Wallaby, Everest Radius, Everest Carat and Everest Jet Lag.

In 1982, horses produced by the Everest Stud were Britain's most successful as substantiated by the British Show Jumping Association's official annual list of leading money winners. The nine horses produced by the Everest Stud that appeared on the list netted a total of £138,000. The best of these was Everest If Ever who had won £32,236 with Nick Skelton in the saddle, followed by Liz who collected £27,267 with Everest Forever.

At the beginning of 1984, the Everest-Edgar combination enjoyed a reputation second to none, with its senior riders Liz and Nick well able to take on and beat the best in the world. Since the Everest connection was initiated a decade and a half earlier, Ted's role had changed from that of international rider to one of Europe's most successful trainers. The advantages of a full-time trainer-manager in attendance at home and on the showgrounds, in a sport where trainers are the exception rather than the rule, cannot be overestimated.

A very tight sense of discipline, loyalty, trust, and hard work is expected from anyone who is part of the Everest entourage on any level. Everyone involved has to be prepared to turn his hand to any task if necessary, as is demonstrated by the fact that when they are at home, it is Nick and Ted who muck out the twenty boxes before breakfast at 8 a.m. each day.

Ted is blunt, afraid of no one, does not suffer fools gladly, and direct and to the point with everyone with whom he deals. The North American adage, 'If you don't do it my way, take the highway,' is both Ted's philosophy and practice. Accordingly, he is quite prepared to tell anyone who fails to meet his high demands to pack their bags, and he means what he says.

As a result, one of the hall-marks of the Everest Stud is that the horses are invariably quite beautifully turned out, the ideal of all would-be teenage stars, while the presence of the Everest riders at a show means that no quarter will be asked or given in competitions that will be hard fought throughout until the red rosette is pinned to the winner's bridle.

CHAPTER ONE

TED EDGAR

As a Surtees-style farmer of the Victorian era, Ted might well have attracted scant attention, but in the drab sameness of twentieth-century England, he enlivens all facets of the equestrian scene like a blazing comet, or as Liz prefers to say, 'like a northern gale'.

A strong, able and fearless horseman with a rumbustious approach to life, he has an irrepressible zest for living and does not want for courage. Strangers could well be deceived by his flamboyant lifestyle which sometimes conceals his vast experience with horses. In some ways a Jekyll and Hyde, his volatile temperament has often landed him in trouble, but conversely, however inconvenient the time or situation, he will go right out of his way to help a friend in trouble.

From his early days, Ted has always had an irascible sense of humour and a taste for the occasional hell-raising. I first heard of him when I was home from school for the holidays and at a South Staffordshire Hunt Pony Club Christmas Ball at The Guildhall in Lichfield. During a lull in the dancing, I heard the rather staid and completely scandalised District Commissioner telling a shocked friend about the terrible, wild goings-on at the equivalent North Warwickshire Pony Club festivities the previous week. The occasion had been rudely interrupted when Ted Edgar had let off some fireworks under the table in the middle of dinner.

Several years later, I was driving home with a friend after seeing a horse that was for sale in Leicestershire. Stopping at a well-known hostelry on the A5 I noticed a huge round hole in the bar window. 'What happened?' I asked the landlord. 'Oh,' he replied casually, as though it happened every day, 'Ted Edgar and his friends were in last night and they threw a barrel of beer through the window.'

And, in the interim, Ted's devil-may-care attitude and sense of fun have not diminished. Colonel Britschgi, sage of the Swiss show-jumping hierarchy, recalls a party in a hotel room in Davos after a competition there, which always took place on the snow, had ended:

Everyone had already had a few drinks and was preparing to tackle a giant pot of the local speciality, cheese fondue, when Ted and Liz arrived. A few minutes later there was a slight scuffle and someone disappeared over the balcony. Ted left the room only to return with a wheelbarrow full of snow which he had brought up in the lift. After an astonishing snowball fight everyone calmed down and began eating the fondue.

Ted's father wanted nothing to do with his son's riding and Ted was taught by his mother, Ethel. By the time he was eight years

Young Ted.

old he was riding a mule to school in the morning, home for lunch and back again to school in the afternoon.

He was soon competing in gymkhanas and small shows near his home at Cryfield Farm, Gibbetts Hill, near Coventry, which is now part of the University of Warwick campus. With a group of older friends he would set off at dawn for a show like the Stratford-on-Avon – a round distance of forty miles – riding one pony and leading another, compete until nine at night and then hack home, singing all the way. In the early days of the Second World War it was still possible to ride over almost anyone's farmland and the merry band went across country barely touching the roads.

Ted's father did not approve of his son competing at gymkhanas and kept stopping him doing so, so Ted ran away. Typically, he went just far enough – to the next farm – only returning a few days later when his father promised to allow him to compete, which he then did as often as possible and in any type of class from gymkhana to best rider to jumping.

Ted's first proper show was the Victory in Europe Show at Stoneleigh, where many years later he was to score so many triumphs. Quickly he progressed to show ponies, being almost unbeatable with the 13.2 h.h. Puzzle and the 14.2 h.h. bay mare Debutante, and with jumping ponies such as Dickie and Tic Tac.

When he was thirteen years old, Ted was expelled from school for smoking 'because I was already heavy for my age and trying to keep my weight down'.

From his teenage days onwards, many of his escapades have been shared by three enduring friends: Lol Weaver, who used to ride against him in point-to-points and who now lives in Coventry; Dave Dick ('Dicko'), not the national hunt jockey but another former point-to-point adversary who is now a garage owner and lives at nearby Harbury; and master showman David Tatlow ('Tatty') with whom he has shared many happy hours following hounds. Hunting is Ted's obsession and when he says, 'I hope to hunt on the day I die,' he is not joking.

Ted began hunting, when he was twelve years old, with the same group of lads with whom he rode to shows, among them· Doug Iggulden, the late Tom McDaide and Johnny Dent. It was towards the end of the war and there was no petrol available so the Tile

Hill Riding and Driving Club was formed: 'You drove the pony to a show in a trap, put a saddle on, competed, put the pony back in the trap and drove home. There was nothing else to do.'

One year a show was put on at Fisher and Ludlow's sports fields in Coventry with a sensational £50 first prize and hopeful winners poured into the ground from miles away. There were boxes parked all over the ground and right down the roads outside – 'no one had ever seen anything like it'.

Debutante has won so many prizes that in contrast to Ted, she is uninterested at the sight of yet another cup.

The post-war increase of interest in show-jumping was clearly demonstrated a year later when the first-ever £200 class was held at Christchurch. The first round started at ten in the morning. The world and his wife were there and at seven in the evening the same round was still in progress. This marathon was eventually won by Pat Smythe on Finality.

Ted rode over seventy winners point-to-pointing and had his first taste of racing when aged fourteen on a fairish lop-eared horse which fell at the first fence dumping the young hopeful bang onto the floor. 'What a useless bastard,' says Ted, describing the horse. This inauspicious start was the precursory race of some highly successful seasons point-to-pointing which would have lasted much longer if Ted, from his early twenties onwards, was not continually fighting a losing battle against his weight.

The Edgar family moved to Leek Wootton when Ted was twelve years old. Tom Edgar bought Elms Farm which was formerly part of Captain Heber-Percy's Guy's Cliffe estate. It was an astute purchase as the land is some of the best in Warwickshire.

At that time, like most farmers, the Edgars did not have a tractor and the farm work was done by heavy horses who often found themselves involved in various unlikely escapades. One took place in the rickyard soon after the family arrived at Elms Farm. Ted and a few of his friends, including Lol Weaver, were all sitting in a transportable hen pen with a horse harnessed up in the shafts, having a quiet smoke out of sight. There was a little window in the front of the pen and suddenly Ted saw his father approaching. This particular horse was a shiverer and wouldn't really go, so Ted gave him a wallop hoping to shoot off through the gate and away from his father across the fields. The move went completely awry: the horse, startled into action, took one huge plunge forward, ripped the entire front out of the hen pen and galloped away down the field with the front of the pen rattling round his heels. The group of young boys were left fully exposed in a cloud of smoke with no possible route of escape as the wrathful Tom Edgar approached. 'There were five of us, we just downed our fags and ran. Oh, he was cross; he really roared at us.'

Ted has one, elder, sister – Marg. As her father's favourite, she was cosseted, usually at Ted's expense. 'Everything she did was right.' It was their joint duty to collect the eggs laid by hens which were kept under arks in the fields. One day Ted was told to move the arks and in doing so hundreds of fowl escaped. Never having been free before the birds went mad, whirring around and flying down to the River Avon. Tom Edgar arrived on the scene. The sparks that flew came not only from his pipe as he admonished his son yet again.

When Ted was sixteen years old, his father saw Warwickshire rider Alan Thompson riding Jane Summers at the Henley-in-Arden Show. By the end of the day Tom Edgar had swopped another mare for Jane Summers and Ted was on his way. The combination were soon programmed onto a series of victories that were to earn Ted the right to wear the Union Jack on his jacket as one of Britain's international show-jumpers. But the fun went on unabated. The first time Jane Summers was taken to compete in

London at the Horse of the Year Show Ted went with Lol. Says Ted, 'We were so keen to get there, pick up the 'phone and tell the birds we were in town, that when we loaded her into our newly acquired cattle truck, we quite forgot there was a big bag of oats inside.' When they arrived they realised that, in their enthusiasm to reach their destination, they had also forgotten to tie up Jane Summers and discovered that she had enjoyed the unexpected windfall and had eaten most of them. Luckily, the mare did not have even a trace of colic.

Deciding they fancied two particular girls, Ted and Lol concluded that the best way to meet them was to kidnap the girls' dog, put it in their horsebox and wait for them to come and look for it. They connected their record player to a nearby lamp-post for power, sat back and waited – all night long. Next day they saw the two girls walk by with a completely different dog from their overnight mongrel companion. They had made a mistake. It should have been a cocker spaniel.

On the showground there was a huge old dinghy which was kept filled with water in case of fire. It was so big that twenty people could get inside. After one evening performance it was upturned by forty hokey-cokey-dancing show-jumpers and their friends, who were then swept on a huge tidal wave down towards some nearby houses. Former show-jumper Derek Kent, now a leading trainer in Hong Kong, and Tom Brake's girlfriends, 'Mad Kath' and 'a huge ginger firebrand', were all part of the hell-bent show-jumping scene at Harringay where, despite such enticing counter-attractions, Jane Summers won the Horse and Hound Cup for Ted. The following year, 1958, which was the final year for the show at Harringay, she shared the Leading Show Jumper of the Year title with Mr Pollard ridden by Pat Smythe. In 1959 she shared the Horse and Hound Cup with John Walmsley's spanking cob, Nugget, clearing a double of gates at 6 feet 1 inch.

Those were the days when jumping held precedence over the clock and horses lasted longer. One reason Jane Summers made her mark was because she was so careful. She was only 15.2 h.h., an unusual mottled chestnut who was partly dappled because she was always so fit. Her only limitation was an aversion to water.

The National Championship at Blackpool also fell to Ted and Jane Summers despite the fact that Tom Edgar tried to stop them competing. This was because he had just bought a sophisticated combine harvest machine which was one of the first to come to England. At the time there was an Irishman working for the Edgars. 'I bet you haven't got one of those in Ireland, have you, Jack?' said Ted as he loaded up the mare. 'Oh, Jesus Christ, yes,' replied Jack. 'We had one twenty years ago but it wasn't automatical.'

Ted drove on to Durham County and won both major classes, together worth £790 which he collected in cash and stashed under the seat of the lorry. He arrived back at 5 a.m., made the mare comfortable, put the rosettes on the kitchen table and fell into bed.

Like most natural horsemen, Ted has an inherent sense of balance, as demonstrated by this fashionable early flamboyant flying position as he went on to win yet another class on the gallant mare Jane Summers. (*Monty*)

At 5.50 a.m. Ted was woken by violent banging on his bedroom door. 'Since you go off to those shows without my permission,' thundered his irate father, not at all elated by his son's National Championship victory, 'you can now get out of bed and milk the cows.'

Ted's victories in 1957 secured him a trip to Holland as a British team member to ride in the Rotterdam CSIO. He made his international debut with style, registering two clear rounds in the Nations' Cup, finished fourth in the Grand Prix and equal first in the Puissance.

Already Ted's eye and growing knowledge were there for the cognoscenti to see. He had played a large part in the production of Mr Pollard for owner John King after the horse, then called Gilpin, was brought out by John Walmsley. He also bought the Argentinian Discutido from show-jumper Ted Williams and later sold him on to David Broome.

Jane Summers was retired at the venerable age of eighteen, at the time when coursebuilder Colonel Jack Ponsonby started building 'desperately long stride tracks with difficult distances, and long stride combinations which her short legs were unable to negotiate'.

Ted, who competed against Germans in Holland, has never changed his opinion of Germany:

> After all our lads were killed in the war, how can I? When I won my first class in Aachen, a German reporter asked me if the English had ever won before in Germany. 'Yes,' I answered, 'we won the war.' I have nothing against Paul Schockemohle – he's my friend, but when I was a kid running about the village I saw people go off to war and come back either as skeletons or shot up with a hand or leg blown off. The new generation doesn't know or want to know about this, so they couldn't understand why I chucked a German off a boat into the sea on my first visit to Rotterdam. But my contemporaries would.

In 1964 Ted and Liz became both engaged and married. 'They did not hang about,' quipped Lol. Ted's father was ill and when his condition began to worsen seriously, Ted gave Liz his horse Jacapo to ride because he had to run the farm. He did not resume serious jumping until he bought Uncle Max in 1968.

Another reason Ted stopped jumping was because he was sus-

Not fancy dress, but Ted competing at Hickstead on Snaffles in the early days with a self-devised head umbrella to combat the driving rain.

pended for his involvement in a minor incident. That was not the first or the last time (a similar occasion when Ted carried the can occurred at Olympia in 1981), but being suspended for two seasons, 1966 and 1967, was a blow. Eventually, former international show-jumper and founder of the Hickstead jumping arena, Dougie Bunn, got Ted's licence back but he had decided not to jump again as he was doing so well on the farm and in cattle dealing.

In 1968, Ted went with Liz to Hickstead, to watch her ride an exceptional novice he'd bought for her called Snaffles. But Snaffles was naughty and the first day she rode him there Liz was eliminated. So Ted rode him the next three days and won each time which re-ignited his own enthusiasm to compete. If Snaffles had gone for Liz, Ted would probably never have returned to the ring.

One day when Ted had sold some cattle very well, David Broome called in mentioning that there was a very good horse in the States called Uncle Max.

Ted asked Uncle Max's owner-rider, 1972 Olympic bronze medallist Neal Shapiro, if he'd sell his horse. Neal asked for £5,000, whereupon Ted smacked Neal's hand and bought him, little dreaming that the horse was to play a key role in the founding of the Everest Stud and totally alter Ted's way of life. After Uncle Max made his final appearance with the US team in Rotterdam, he was brought back to England by Johnny Kidd from whom Ted collected him.

Uncle Max was a grey, former rodeo horse and initially he fought his new rider as he had been taught at the 6-Bar-6 Ranch in Wyoming. He was a jumper of enormous character and would only perform to an audience, as Ted explains:

> If he went to a show and there was no one there, he would do nothing. He would kick the fences out, even in a £1,000 class, if no one was watching. I tell you, he would have thirty faults. But at an ordinary show, with several hundred people watching, where he might only have been jumping for a fiver, he would go to the lights. He liked it best indoors when the crowds started clapping, and he would buck as we came into the ring. He loved the limelight but there was no way I could ride him round the farm at home, he didn't enjoy that at all.

By October, the combination had come to terms. After Ted had been placed fourth in the Foxhunter Championship on Snaffles at the Horse of the Year Show, Uncle Max gave the crowd a taste of triumphs to come and won the Dick Turpin Stakes, an all-gate class, on the Wednesday. Ted phoned home the following morning

ABOVE Uncle Max, the dynamic former US rodeo horse who fired Ted with the ambition to return to competition in the late 1960s and caught the imagination of the crowd with his amazing bucking style. (*Monty*)

BELOW Major Reg Whitehead, course designer at the Bath and West Show in the 1960s and early 1970s, reckoned he could build a course that only M'Lord could jump. Here M'Lord and Ted are substantiating his statement by winning the Somerset AIT in 1973. (*Monty*)

only to be told that his mother had died a few minutes earlier at
7.30 a.m. That night he won the Puissance with a dazzling display
of explosive power.

Like so many riders before him, Ted had set his heart on winning
the King's Cup, with Uncle Max, but then, as now, the only way
an English rider could compete was by being in a British team or
by winning an AIT. Ted managed to get selected for Aachen, and
then, to qualify for the King's Cup, had to beg Douglas Bunn to
let him ride Uncle Max in the Nations' Cup although he knew the
course would not suit him.

Ted's forebodings were right. Uncle Max turned head over heels
in the second round in the ring, came out on three legs and looked
as though he'd never jump again. However, within a week he was
back in action and only ten days after his fall a proud Ted was
holding the huge, gold, St George and the Dragon, King's Cup
trophy.

In that year, 1969, Uncle Max achieved seventeen second placings, including that gained at the Hamburg Derby, and four wins,
namely, the King's Cup, Leading Show Jumper of the Year at the
Horse of the Year Show, a £25 class at Gloucester and one local
£15 class.

Throughout 1970 Uncle Max was consistently in the money, but
by 1971 his back legs were virtually finished.

Ted's interest in show-jumping was completely resurrected and
the farm re-organised, being devoted totally to sheep and to the
growing of the horses' hay and oats. Uncle Max's spectacular
successes had attracted sponsorship from Everest Double Glazing
and, as Uncle Max had retired, Snaffles was the first horse to carry
the company prefix.

In the early and mid-seventies, Ted's main object was to find
horses good enough to carry the Everest name and, as his protégé
Nick Skelton matured, ones that they both could ride. The problem
was that he thought the horses he bought for himself would be too
big for Nick, who weighed only eight stone, and so he found it
difficult to mount them both on the same horses.

One horse Ted bought was the big mare Louisiana. When he
couldn't get a tune out of her he put up Nick, who 'flew around on
her like a hero'. 'The man can ride these sizeable horses,' Ted
suddenly realised, never having given him the chance before. After

Ted waiting with Everest Wallaby just before a class, having just worked in the horse for Liz. Liz acknowledges Ted as being totally responsible for all her wins with this horse. (*Evening Mail*)

that, Nick progressed from strength to strength with any horse. Prior to that, Nick had almost exclusively ridden Maybe with Ted occasionally schooling the horse to keep him in line.

Among the horses that Ted bought at this period were Jet Lag and Lastic. Nick only got the ride on Lastic because Ted broke his leg. The accident happened at the Royal Agricultural Show at Stoneleigh. Up till then, and for a year afterwards, he had no intention whatsoever of swapping over his role from competitor and part-time trainer, to full-time trainer.

On that fateful July day, Ted was attempting to jump a combination which was constructed adjacent to the packed grandstand:

I'm not sure if Lastic actually stopped or hesitated at the middle element, but he tipped up after jumping a corner of the fence, hitting a pole, which swung round and hit me hard on the knee. The next thing I knew, I was on the floor. I looked down and there was my knee-cap which had busted through my breeches, half was way down the front of my calf, and the other half, way up my thigh. I remember sitting there unable to move. 'Banky' [Yorkshire owner Trevor Banks] rushed in to help, followed by a mass of people who collected round me. What did he say but, 'You silly idiot, what are you doing sitting there? Don't you know there's a show on?'

Ted was rushed away in an ambulance to Warwick General Hospital and 'Banky' insisted on going with him. Ted's left knee-cap was smashed straight in half. He was operated on the day after he was admitted and he discharged himself the following day, only forty-eight hours after the accident. 'I gave orders to turn all my horses out into the field. But only a few hours later I thought, well, that's a mistake, just because I'm grounded for a while . . . the best policy would be to let Nick ride them.'

So Ted sent his grooms to fetch his horses back from the field and on the Sunday following the Royal, Nick competed on them and won a class each on Lastic, Jet Lag and Amigo. As soon as he arrived home Ted decided that he couldn't bear the plaster cast on his leg. 'I wanted to have a look at my knee and see what was going on. The doctors had said it would take six or eight weeks to mend.'

The pain from his leg, especially at night, was unbearable, so Ted rang physiotherapist Jack Riley, who has looked after him since he was eighteen or nineteen years old, and asked him to cut the plaster of Paris from his leg.

Jack was 'frit' to death as the plaster had been put on in hospital and said he couldn't come and help me. So, I waited till Liz went out, got a cross-saw and did the job myself. Then I asked a 'chippy' [carpenter] from Kenilworth to make me a cradle to stop me bending my leg when I was in bed at night. He used the wood from a crib-biter's cradle and it worked very well. After that I spent a lot of time in the swimming pool, which took all the swelling out of my leg, and wore only an elastic bandage.

Three weeks later I went to the hospital and the doctors put on another plaster, so I sawed it off as soon as I arrived home, put on a bandage as before and continued my own treatment.

Gradually Ted's knee-cap mended and he started to ride again but

FACING PAGE
Ted and Grandpa. All hunters benefit from show-jumping experience and Grandpa certainly has plenty of that. Seen here competing with Ted in 1979. (*Bob Langrish*)

not to show-jump, as the outdoor season was almost over and the World Cup series only in its infancy. Instead he decided to indulge himself and hunted all winter.

While Nick was getting on well with Ted's horses and setting a new British high jump record at Olympia in December 1979, Ted was not worried that he was not show-jumping. But, in 1980, when Grandpa would not go for Nick, Ted took him over and started competing again. Across the border at the Royal Welsh Show at Builth Wells, before he went into the ring with Grandpa, Ted had a premonition that he would break his other knee.

I told Nick before I went into the ring that no way should I ride that day. I knew I would smash up my other knee, but everyone stood and laughed at me. I went into the ring, where there was a double of an upright in and a parallel out. As Grandpa jumped in, I felt something go bang and pulled him out before the parallel. When I reached the collecting ring I said, 'I've smashed my other knee,' and no one would believe me. I couldn't bend my leg at all, but everyone still laughed.

At last a helpful girl appeared out of the blue. She instantly realised that Ted was not kidding and that his knee was, in all probability, broken. She found people to carry him back to his horsebox which was parked a long way up the side of a hill, and also organised a doctor, who confirmed that Ted's knee was broken. Liz was contacted and had to drive down from Leek Wootton to fetch him home that night.

The following day, he took the by now well-trodden path to the Warwick General Hospital where the surgeon told him he had broken his other knee in exactly the same way as before, by splitting his patella. The knee was re-set and encased in plaster and gradually mended. Ted has never jumped in the ring since then.

And so, by accident rather than design, 1980 proved a turning point in Ted's career and he took on the role of full-time trainer in the Everest Stud. From that moment onwards, the Stud's already portentous run of successes continued to develop and escalate. Having a full-time groundsman is a big advantage because a rider can by no means always assess why he has made an error. And when that trainer is also able to jump on to the horse's back at the

FACING PAGE
Life at the Rio Grande.

ABOVE LEFT Liz making coffee in the kitchen. (*Akhtar Hussein*)

ABOVE RIGHT Liz and Ted leading Halo up the drive through the ranch gate. (*Akhtar Hussein*)

BELOW In the centre aisle of the stables, Liz, Halo, Nick, Ted and the dogs. (*Akhtar Hussein*)

The intrepid Ted, out hunting with the North Cotswold, makes nothing of some wide brambles. (*Jim Meads*)

drop of a hat and discipline or balance him, the benefits are obvious.

*   *   *

To understand the motivation and colour of Ted's life is difficult. The following reminiscences about four other facets of his career may help to illustrate the fun and complexity of his character.

HUNTING

Hunting is unquestionably Ted's favourite pastime, in fact a compulsive passion. One fellow hunt member, aptly commenting after a particularly testing day in Ted's wake, recalls, 'To ride to hounds after Ted is the equivalent of riding the wall of death.'

Few, if any, obstacles will stop Ted. One day, out with the Atherstone, Ted, who was mounted on a slowish horse, came across the rest of the hunt after a long and testing gallop. The field had stopped and were anxiously contemplating a pair of solid railway gates all too close to a canal.

'Out the way!' he shouted, and two neat leaps later was on his way while someone dismounted to open the gates for lesser mortals.

*   *   *

One September when Nick was eighteen years old and feeling very pleased with himself after a marvellous season during which he'd won the European Junior Championship, Ted recalls how he took him out cub hunting with the Heythrop:

> Nick was out there with his knees up, just about to show the Heythrop how to operate, when Tatty cantered up alongside him, put his hand under his foot and jumped him off, straight out of the saddle, point-to-point style, and I had to catch the horse which had galloped off and gone spare. All this in full view of the field.
>
> Three months later, Tatty came to buy a horse from me. I told Nick to ride with David down the field, so he could try the horse and give it a few pops. They set off round the farm and jumped one or two places. Then I saw Nick driving Tatty straight towards the end of a fence where there is an old pit on the landing side which you can't see on take-off. I had no chance to get across the fields fast enough to stop him, and there's Skelton jumping a hundred yards away, quite safely, watching Tatty ride straight into his trap and tip 'a over t' into the pit, like I have never seen. How Tatty did not break his own or my horse's neck I do not know. Never before or after have I seen such a tip-up.

Then Skelton had a nasty moment as Tatty lay absolutely motionless on the ground. He rode over, worried that Tatty was badly hurt. As he got to the pit Tatty suddenly sat up roaring with laughter and said, 'You got me back.'

*   *   *

One day David Tatlow rang Ted to see if he was going hunting the next day with the Warwickshire and Ted replied in the affirmative. When David arrived at the meet, another member of the hunt told him Prince Charles was expected to join them at midday. But by three o'clock, when the field had already seen some fair sport, the royal visitor still hadn't appeared.

Tatty got more and more worked up, Ted remembers:

His knickers were in a right twist by the time he heard HRH was down a nearby road. There was a five-barred gate – she was a big old iron one – between us and the road, and about thirty-five top hunting people left. Tatty went to open the gate in front of the field while the Master was casting hounds, trying to waste time while waiting for Prince Charles. Tatty struggled to open the gate four times without success. 'Mind out, Tatty,' I shouted and he pulled back. I gave my horse a big kick in the belly, popped over the gate and trotted up the road to find Prince Charles. Tatty could have killed me. 'Thank you very much, you ignorant bastard,' he shouted after me, and the whole of the hunting field exploded with laughter.

I found Prince Charles and we joined the field. For a whole hour Tatty cut me dead and refused to speak to me. He was furious. Prince Charles said to me, 'What's wrong with David, have you fallen out with him?' 'I've just done something wrong to him,' I explained, 'and I shall ring and apologise tonight.' I didn't do it on purpose, I just thought it was a bad gate to open, so it'd be easier to pop over it. I didn't mean to make Tatty look two inches tall. He really took the hump but he did manage to laugh about it later.

*   *   *

Ted was hunting with the Heythrop another day when Prince

Charles was out and some of the field found themselves in a very awkward railed corner:

Prince Charles turned to Australian show-jumper Kevin Bacon and said, 'You're a show-jumping man, give us a lead over these rails.' Kevin's horse wasn't very good at all so Kevin turned to Prince Charles and, not knowing who he was, said, 'If you want to jump the bastard, you jump it, I'm not going to.' With that he left Prince Charles standing looking at the rails. Soon afterwards I said to Kevin, 'Did you realise who spoke to you?' 'I don't care if it was the King of England,' Kevin said disbelievingly, 'I'm not going to try and jump them rails with this bloody thing I'm on today.'

*   *   *

Ted rates highly his friend the former football player, manager and now television expert, Jimmy Hill. Jimmy loves his hunting but to begin with he did everything wrong, as Ted explains:

He didn't realise that even if you go out to dinner or drinking with a Master of Foxhounds the night before a hunt, you do not call him George, Jack, Harry or whatever when you see him at the meet the next morning. You must say, 'Good morning, Master,' and show some respect. But at first, Jimmy kept calling the Master by his christian name and I had to keep correcting him. Then Jimmy said he was going to try to become an MFH himself so everyone would have to call him Master.

Bill Shaw Fox, who was Secretary of the North Warwickshire Hunt, turned to Jimmy one morning while we waited as hounds were drawing a covert and said, 'You know, Hill, I was looking at you over the dinner table last night and if ever you fall off, with that big chin of yours, you'd plough the blasted field without even needing a plough and tractor.' 'If I could call you Bill instead of Mr Secretary, I could answer that observation, but I can't talk to you properly until I've taken off my hunting clothes,' replied Jimmy, who by now understood the form.

*   *   *

Ted first met Jimmy Hill at a pub in Coventry after a Coventry
City football match. Although this was a comparatively recent
occasion, they have become firm friends, despite Ted's first im-
pressions:

> Coventry City were playing well at the time and Hill had just
> been appointed manager. As I sat having my drink I saw this
> fellow with a ruddy great long chin walk in. Someone introduced
> us and Hill said he'd like to learn to ride. I, like an idiot, said,
> 'Come on over some time and I'll teach you.'

One of Jimmy Hill's first days following hounds. He is flanked by Liz and Ted on
a wet November morning. (*Monty*)

Ted had not meant unannounced at 6 a.m. the following morning. 'Oh, Christ,' Ted said to Liz, 'that bloke I told you about last night has turned up. The best thing we can do is to get out a horse, put him up and get his backside and knees so sore that he won't bother us any more.'

But Ted had completely underestimated Hill. After an hour non-stop on the lungeing rein, his knees and seat were red raw and desperately inflamed. 'He dropped his trousers to show us the mess, so I drenched the sore parts in methylated spirits. His language got a bit blue and he wasn't at all pleased. Great, I thought, that will be goodbye, the end of him.'

Again, Ted had not got the measure of Hill who turned up at the same time the next day with large plasters on his knees and seat – plus his pyjama trousers for extra protection. 'Christ, Liz,' said Ted, 'this fellow is here for life. If he'll stick yesterday's treatment, he'll stick anything.' From then on, Hill seldom missed a morning's lesson, arriving at 5.55 a.m. each day in Ted's yard, to ride until 8 a.m. Then he had a quick cup of coffee and some toast, left at 8.15 a.m. and drove straight to his office to run Coventry City.

The first time Ted took Jimmy out hunting he told him to follow as best he could and try not to let him (Ted) get out of sight. Quite early on, Ted jumped over a succession of six five-barred gates, and as he looked back over his shoulder on landing over the last one, to see where Jimmy was, the newcomer to the scene almost landed on top of him. 'That was fun,' said Jimmy. 'Where do we go now?' The pupil lacked nothing of the spirit of his master.

Another firm and enduring friendship had begun in a most unconventional way. To this day, Hill hunts as often as his television and other business commitments permit, and now keeps two or three hunters at his house near Stow-on-the-Wold.

POINT-TO-POINTING

Ted's point-to-pointing career carried him first past the post on a wide variety of mounts including his father's Boddington Hill and Paul Pry, and Sid Sutton's flying grey Prince Neron – 'Which felt like sitting on a gate with the bridle on the post; I just couldn't hold the horse.' Somewhat unconventionally Prince Neron was

On their way to the winners' enclosure after winning at the Harkaway Club Meeting at Chaddesley Corbett in 1963, Ted and the late Mrs Leonard Carver's Culleenhouse. (*Monty*)

largely trained on a horse walker while his owner was busy milking his cows. Other horses included Mrs Leonard Carver's Culleenhouse, Homefinder, and ESB who went on to win the National, and the late Harry Barton's Lawless. Ted rode five times at Aintree, desperately hoped to ride ESB in the National and was more than disappointed when Dave Dick, who'd fallen in the previous race, got up, still took the ride and went on to triumph in 1956, the year when the Queen Mother's Devon Loch faltered on the run-in.

Of all the famous point-to-pointers he rode, Ted describes the little horse Paul Pry as 'the tops'. Ted and his father bought him at Stockton Sales from Archie Thomlinson. *Tom Edgar gives record price of 800 guineas* recorded the *Horse and Hound*. At the time it was an unbelievable figure.

In Coronation Year, 1953, Ted and Lol set off for Larkhill with Paul Pry and he won the first of over twenty races for his new stable. No respecter of his new jockey, the 15.3 h.h. bay gelding kicked Ted off any morning he felt so inclined and was usually turned out in the field after a race.

One of the first tracks Ted rode at was Chesterton, near the late John Thorne's stud. One day he was riding a 20-1 shot there when a jockey friend of his who had hit hard times came up and said he had backed Ted and himself to finish first and second. Ted took an early lead and when he had jumped four fences he heard his friend come up behind shouting: 'You needn't worry, they've all gone through the rails.' Ted takes up the story:

> He'd only pushed our six rivals right out of the race, and there was a big enquiry afterwards. At the last fence my friend's horse was exhausted and fell but he remounted, finished and made a fortune.

*   *   *

The dieting was desperate: 'It just killed me always having to lose weight.' Even from the early days when he worked out regularly in a gym at Leamington with former world middleweight boxing champion, Randolph Turpin, Ted faced an agonising fight against his weight. Friends calling in the evening at Elms Farm were quite used to chatting to Ted as he lay like a huge boiled lobster in a bright pink towel on his bed, recovering after steaming in an overhot bath to try and knock off weight for an imminent race. It was his continuing battle against avoirdupois, coupled with the fact that with first prizes as low as £10, point-to-pointing was a desperately expensive sport, that finally decided Ted to hang up his racing boots.

On a race day at Chaddesley Corbett, Martin Tate, who is now a successful National Hunt trainer, was in charge of the scales. Ted went to weigh in rather late and was a most unusual two pounds under weight. 'Just a minute, Edgar. Stand still, please,' said Tate and disappeared. Then, reappearing five minutes later, said he had gone to have a bet. 'He realised straightaway that if I could do the weight, I thought I'd win, and I did at 25-1.'

One year Ted hoped to ride the wild Prince Neron in the Dudley

Cup but when he arrived at Chaddesley Corbett, the horse's owner, Sid Sutton, wouldn't run him in the race. Instead the horse started in the Adjacent Hunts with a seven pounds penalty and won in a time eight seconds faster than the Dudley Cup winner. It was the sole time Ted ever carried a weight cloth in his life.

David Tatlow says of his friend and erstwhile point-to-point rival:

> Ted was a very underrated rider, a real bold lad on a front runner. If he were not constantly overweight, he would probably have been champion . . . and he had a little way of surreptitiously slipping a piece of chewing-gum under the scales to be sure he made the weight.

*   *   *

The only time Ted was ever scared was at the Pytchley when he was riding along between Tony Rogers, who won so many races with Mythical Ray, and David Tatlow. Over one jump Ted's horse fired him up into the air and he landed back in the plate with one leather twisted round. As they galloped on Ted said to Rogers, 'If my horse falls my leg will be pulled out of its socket.' 'Sort it out then,' he replied. Somehow Ted got his foot out of the stirrup and disentangled himself, negotiating the next fence in an extremely precarious style, then accelerated forward to win.

*   *   *

Ted often had to rush to get to the races:

> 'What about the day we went to Wincanton in the big Jag and the coppers had me for running over some ducks on the way? I came round a corner at seventy miles an hour and these ducks were crossing the road. Suddenly the air was clouded with feathers. Shortly afterwards a copper stopped me saying, 'Did you see those ducks you ran over a mile or so back?' 'What ducks?' I replied. 'Well, sir,' he said, moving round to the front of the car, 'you've got one on your radiator.'

*   *   *

The Croome-qualified Knight's Frolic had never won a race, had fallen several times and had been ridden by almost everyone when his owner Mr Taylor asked Ted if he would ride his horse the following week. Ted went and galloped Knight's Frolic, agreed to do so and told Mr Taylor that his horse would win.

> The old boy got very excited. 'Oh, my God,' he said, 'I've never had a winner in my life,' and he rang me every morning and night from then onwards until the day of the race.
>
> The races were at Lowsonford near Henley-in-Arden and Tatlow came up saying he had a good horse and would win. I told him there and then to stop his horse and go for it next week, because I wasn't going to be beat.
>
> Mr Taylor came up and said, 'I've had £2 on you, Ted, at eight to one.' 'Then go back and make it £100 because I won't get caught.' I won by twenty lengths, the others couldn't get near us.
>
> 'I've got to buy you a drink, Ted,' said the happy owner. 'I only want a beer,' I replied, and was promptly given two cases.
>
> The old chap couldn't believe he had won and when the Master, Tom Bates, went to award him the Cup, he started to cry and his teeth fell out. Poor old boy.

Ted won two more races on Knight's Frolic but never rode him after that because of increasing weight problems.

*   *   *

Those were the good old days. However, Ted well remembers when, at the age of about nineteen, he was 'done' in a race by a certain well-respected Army major.

> We were galloping along side by side when he suddenly put his hand under my foot and fired me straight out of the saddle. As I walked back to the changing room he said, 'Keep to yourself what I just did, boy. You'll learn all these little tricks yourself in time.'

*   *   *

Cliff Toone's father, the late Percy Toone, used to stutter a lot. At one Atherstone meeting, at Clifton-on-Dunsmore, after his horse King's Crest had won the members' heavyweight division carrying fourteen stone seven pounds, he approached Ted to see if he would ride the same horse in the Maiden Race later that day where it only had to carry twelve stone seven pounds. Ted agreed and was beaten by half a length, by Dick Black on Harry Barton's Lawless.

As we walked into the paddock towards the winning enclosure, past a group of ladies and gentlemen, old man Toone said to me, 'You would have won if you hadn't been p-p-p-p-p-?...' Everyone quickly ducked down and looked away thinking he was about to say something else, but what he was trying to say was, '... if you hadn't been penalised for King's Crest's earlier win.'

At another Atherstone meeting, it was the unfortunate Lol who inadvertently shattered his own and his friend's plans. They had saved a horse for a particular day, run it twice and got it right for Ted.

Lol, the big betting man, went down and put on all our money – £20 – £2 from each of us including bets from Tatty and Tony Rogers, so at 10 to 1 we were each going to win a fortune – and there was no limit as to what we could do with £200. Lol was riding in the same race and what did he do but shoot out of the gate to the front on some camel. Four from home, Lol didn't start to come back to us so we got worried. 'Jump off, you berk' I shouted, but he just went farther ahead. So I gave my horse a crack on the backside and had a cut at him and failed, then I told Tony to go up and get him, but it was all to no avail. Tatlow tried too, but got nowhere and Lol won.

'I'm sorry about that,' the jokey devil shouted over his shoulder, 'but I couldn't stop.' Lol had lost all his friends' money on the aptly named Victory Boy and we cursed and swore at him for two hours afterwards.

*   *   *

One spring at the Pytchley point-to-points Dave Dick had been drinking cider in the car all the way because he had nothing to ride and had become quite merry. Ted recalls that

There was a young jockey at the races with a camera, which was unusual because, in those days, only toffs had cameras. He came into the changing tent with his camera round his neck, took it off, hung it up and changed into his silks. Dicko took the camera and filled the film with shots of all the jockeys with their trousers down, and even someone in the cloakroom. When Dicko finished the reel, he put the camera back where he had found it.

The camera owner was 'real posh'. He turned up at another meeting three weeks later. There had been an awful scene at the chemist's shop where he had taken the film to be developed and he had been accused of taking dirty pictures. 'Mummy and Daddy' were very cross and told him he must have some very unsuitable racing friends.

*   *   *

In the early seventies, soon after Liz and Ted were married, Ted was riding the point-to-point mare, Miss Winwick, which belonged to my father. A chestnut mare with large lop ears, she was able, but difficult to train. One season when she was right she was travelled up to Flagg Moor in Derbyshire with much optimism for her success. Unfortunately, half-way through the races thick fog descended on the course, which was set in stone-walled country, and the meeting was abandoned before Miss Winwick's race.

At the time, Ted's fight against his weight was critical so he had a special saddle made which weighed a bare pound. (A normal saddle would weigh about nine pounds.) It was a mere leaf of a saddle requiring superb balance to stay in the plate.

Enthusiasm was justifiably high the following week when Miss Winwick and Ted set off for the Albrighton Meeting. The pair came into the last fence with far more in hand than the remaining two challengers, placed one on each side. Then disaster struck as her two rivals shut her out in mid-flight. Ted was shot off, breaking a bone in his lower leg, while Miss Winwick hit the ground with a horrid thump and lay winded.

Ted has never lacked for courage and the following Saturday the team was back on the road again, bound for the Albrighton Woodland Point-to-Points at Chaddesley Corbett in Worcester-

Ted has a clear lead on Mr Bernard Martin's mare Miss Winwick. (*Findlay Davidson*)

shire. Ted, who had insisted on carrying on racing, rode valiantly with his broken leg strapped up, and Miss Winwick finished an honourable fourth in a field of almost thirty starters.

THE LAW

One year Ted and his friend Dave Dick went to Finmere Show which was run partly in aid of the Injured Jockeys' Fund, so there were jockeys and bookmakers present as well as show-jumpers. People were betting as to who could climb a flagpole in the middle of a big tent. Ted managed to get only half-way up.

A bookie offered 10–1 that no one would succeed and Dick put on £10 that someone would reach the top. Along came the famous Australian Olympic Three-Day Event gold medallist, Bill Roycroft – who Ted reckoned 'had to be seventy years old if he was a day' – and he climbed right up and came down again without any trouble at all. A large crowd had assembled and the entire tent was thrown into uproar. Then the bookie completely refused to pay out Dick's winnings, so after a heated discussion Ted and Dick went outside and sat on the bookie's Rolls-Royce.

When the bookie came along with two friends 'Dicko and I had a bit of sport and flattened the three of them. With that we decided to hop it, and we jumped into our car and drove off, but we were caught.' The next day the newspaper headlines screamed out, *Show-jumper charged with inflicting grievous bodily harm.* Ted and Dick had to go to court, where a large number of bookies and show-jumpers had assembled.

Ted recollects that Miles Gosling, formerly a deputy senior steward of the Jockey Club, was on the bench: 'He gave the bookie a rousting, and Dicko and I got one too, but nothing else happened. He talked to us like three school kids and then dismissed us out of court.' Dicko and Ted finished up in a pub that night with the bookie but they never succeeded in getting the money they were owed.

*   *   *

One evening in April 1982, Ted had been out having a drink with 'the lads' when he decided he fancied some fish and chips, so he called at Kenilworth on the way home to buy some. Coming back through Castle Gutter, which is only a mile from Leek Wootton,

> A copper stopped me because the backboard of the little pick-up van I was driving had come down. 'Have you been drinking?' he asked. 'Yes,' I replied, so he breathalised me. Then he said I hadn't blown properly into the bag and went to get another one. I hopped off, ran through a gateway and away over the fields. But the sole came off my shoe, I fell flat on my face, and the copper, who was following, caught me and took me in.

Ted's solicitor, Roger Blakemore, who lives in the hamlet of Arlescote at the foot of Edgehill, has a partner called Geoff Barrett who has proved to be expert at extracting Ted from tight, seemingly inescapable, corners. Ted was so certain he would be convicted that he decided to take a horse to court in a horsebox to ensure that he could get home, riding if necessary.

Everyone said it was my own fault and that I deserved to get done. Also they were far too busy moving house from 'Ponderosa' to 'Rio Grande' to worry about me. 'Blast you,' I said as I loaded the horse into the lorry. 'I'll ride the bleeder back if you won't help me and then I shall buy a float and get around that way.'

The horse stood in the lorry all day and I nearly got pinched for leaving the box in the car park near the court in Leamington Spa. The policeman who was on duty there when I came out said that as I was lucky enough to get off one charge, he might as well let me off the other and told me to get off the place as fast as possible. You should have seen everyone's expression when I drove home up the drive, no one could believe I still had my licence.

Geoff Barrett had achieved a miracle.

*   *   *

The only time Ted was convicted for drinking and driving was in 1975 after he'd been to a boxing match at the Hilton Hotel:

I wasn't drinking much at the time because I was dieting hard so I had only had three glasses of wine with David Mould – at the time he was the Queen Mother's steeplechase jockey. I left at 10.45 p.m. and drove home down the motorway. A copper stopped me, produced a breathaliser and said I was doing 135 mph.

But when Ted arrived in court, the police dropped the speeding charge and went for the drunken one (he was marginally over the limit). Ted maintains that the speed quoted was wrong because 'the car I was driving couldn't go anywhere near that fast'. On 19th December, 1975 Ted lost his licence for twelve months.

THE ENTERTAINER

Like Harvey Smith, who has built himself a reputation for his night-club act, singing, and telling jokes, Ted has established some

notoriety as an entertainer, and with his quick turn of phrase for
the unexpected, is often hilariously funny. Although he seldom
makes any appearance in public in this way except for charity, one
notable exception is Olympia where he regularly turns out to help
Show Director Raymond Brooks-Ward with his Christmas ex-
travaganza as Colonel-in-Chief of the Camels.

The camels, lent by Mary Chipperfield of the famous circus
family, are one of the most popular acts in the show, no less Ted's
on-going feud with camel Rosie:

> Rosie is a right bitch, she snarls at me all the time and often tries
> to bite. When we first had the camels at Olympia, I, like an idiot,
> started acting the fool and Brooks-Ward suggested I got myself
> into the arena with the camels for a bit of fun. But it was no
> joke, we led them into the arena and, once there, they wouldn't
> run, they wouldn't do anything. So we got two bass brooms, to
> make them shift a bit, and one turned on me. Later I found out
> that her name was Rosie. The other chased Malcolm Pyrah right
> out of the place and he refused to come back. And this was only
> a rehearsal.

Although the camels are so difficult to handle, they have proved a
great draw for the public. Each year, three months before the
show, Ted gets a reminder from Raymond Brooks-Ward telling
him he is detailed for the camels. Ted finds it surprising that the
camels are so very popular and that show-business personalities
and people from all walks of life are so keen to ride them.

Ted is adamant that show-jumping today is, to a degree, show-
business, and that those involved have a duty to put something
back into the sport that is their life-blood.

One of the most amusing scenes at Olympia involved the Irish
international Con Power, 'a big fellow, at well over six feet tall'.
'Typical Irishman that he is, he believed that Pyrah and Skelton
would be true to their word when they told him to go up a ladder,
and wait there for a camel to be brought along to him.' Con was
still a captain in the Irish Army at the time. 'Do your Irish Army
salute,' Ted advised, 'the crowd will love it. We'll bring a camel to
you and you can easily jump onto the animal from the top step.'
So Con climbs up the steps, does his salute wearing the Irish Army

uniform and fetches the house down. 'We never went near him with a camel, never took any notice of him and he stood to attention while we went through the whole camel routine.'

On the way back to the collecting ring, driving the camels back to their stables, Pyrah said to the audience, 'Look at that big dozy Irishman, still stood up there.' The whole crowd screamed with laughter as Pyrah and Ted walked out of the arena leaving Con behind. 'Oh, by Jesus, Malcolm,' shouted Con, 'I'll have you when I get down!' Says Ted, 'Imagine Pyrah, four foot nothing, and Con over six feet high shouting at each other.'

Coursebuilder Alan Ball watches Nick jumping a fence on Rosie. (*Kit Houghton*)

Ted believes that the beauty of the exercise is that all the international riders come to ride the camels – Pyrah, Skelton, Ricketts, Fletcher, they all have a go. He says, 'They are in there for the laugh and the crack, trying to wreak havoc, by tripping one another up, including me, the Colonel, which all adds to the fun.'

*   *   *

The Olympia fancy dress competition is almost always a wow and provides a brief interlude when even the most solemn and dedicated show-jumpers let their hair down. Probably the funniest occasion was when Nick and Ted put on a double-act. Ted cast himself in the role of a squalling, petulant, large pink baby, with Nick as his skinny nursemaid.

The idea evolved from the fact that Captain Mark Phillips and Princess Anne were expecting their first baby, Master Peter Phillips. As Ted knows Captain Phillips very well, he knew he would take the joke in good heart. Ted and Nick were determined to win, as they had done the previous year, and Liz was detailed to provide all the props, which included a pram, some baby powder and her pet corgi.

Wearing only a white nappy, Ted was a very naughty baby who sorely tried his unfortunate nursemaid, screaming and throwing all his toys out of his pram. Trevor Banks was in on the act and when Nick got Ted out of the pram, 'to do all those things they do to babies', it was arranged that he would come in with a bucket of flour and throw it all over Ted because he wouldn't stand having the baby powder put on. Ted recalls what happened,

In came 'Banky' saying, 'Get out of the bloody road, Skelton,' under his breath. As I was lying on the floor, I didn't see him walking across the arena behind me, but all the crowd did. Then he drowned me with the contents of the bucket – and Jesus, it wasn't flour as we'd planned but ice-cold water!

The house dissolved with glee as Ted leapt to his feet and chased Nick and Banks out of the arena.

*   *   *

The year Master Peter Phillips was born, Ted and Nick changed roles in the
Olympia Fancy Dress Competition. Cast: Nick as Master Phillips, Ted as his
Nanny, the late Caroline Bradley as Captain Mark Phillips. (*Findlay Davidson*)

It was to help David Tatlow in April 1983, that Ted first reappeared
in the ring on a horse after a gap of four years, at the Birmingham
International. David had won the Working Hunter Championship
on the Irish heavyweight chestnut, The Senator, but had to leave
because he had five runners at a point-to-point meeting the afternoon of the overall championship. Thus he needed someone to
ride the horse for him.

'The horse moved like a dream,' enthused Ted. His joint owner,
Mr Trevithick, rang Ted the following morning and said, 'You
don't know me, but thank you very much . . . you did a great job
and before the day is over, there will be some Scotch on your
table.' A bottle duly arrived. Before the Championship Ted said to
Nick, 'Listen, when I go in the ring I don't go in to mess about, I
go in to win.' The Senator went quite as well for Ted as for
master-showman Tatlow. Predictably Ted had not missed a trick.
He really looked the part, as smart as paint with his hunting stock
tied to perfection, gold pin, kid gloves, and boots so polished you
could comb your hair in them. 'What a situation to be in, on a
perfectly produced horse like that.'

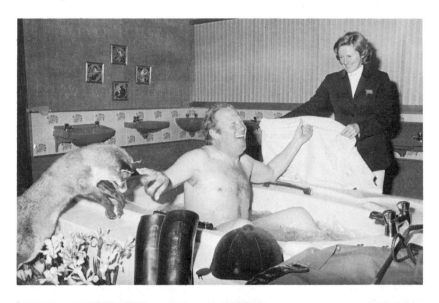

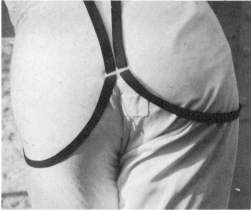

TOP Only Ted would want to test the comfort of a jacuzzi in the middle of the Twyford showroom.

ABOVE LEFT In days of yore, when times were poor. Ted relaxing between classes at Cannes, 1971.

ABOVE RIGHT This pretty lady is Ted plus wig.

CHAPTER TWO

LIZ EDGAR

Liz's first memories of starting to ride are at Mount Ballan, near Chepstow in Monmouthshire, where the family lived in a mansion which had a long drive. Her father, Fred Broome, bought the property from a Mrs Cropper, and, as it was occupied at the time by the Land Army, the family moved from Rhiwbina, where Liz was born, and lived temporarily in a house at nearby Caldicot.

In 1949, they moved in when the house became vacant. Mr Broome's family originally came from South Wales where they were 'fruiters'. He left Cardiff when he decided to alter course and farm instead.

Mrs Broome, who is known as 'Millie', came from Scotland. She

A diminutive Liz riding side-saddle as to the manner born on her brother David's jumping pony, Coffee, at Chepstow in 1953.

met her husband-to-be when her father, a superintendent for an-cient buildings, was transferred to Cardiff. Liz is one of a family of four. Her elder brother, David, is a former World Show Jumping Champion, and she has a younger sister and brother, Mary and Fred, both of whom have competed with success.

Liz clearly recalls one of her first efforts at trotting when her pony shot up a bank throwing her into a thorn bush. 'After that, I wouldn't trot or canter any more. Next, I remember Dad putting me on the lunge one day and making the pony trot, and us going round and round. From that day on, everything was all right; I was cured.'

From eight to twelve years old, she was jumping at best two ponies in 12.2 h.h. classes and learning the rudiments of the sport. The ponies were all Welsh and very cheap. One of the nicest was Skylark, a bay mare saved from slaughter who cost a song and was really kind. Liz recalls those early days:

> Dad went to all the shows with me; he was lorry-driver-cum-trainer and also rode himself. There weren't 13.2 h.h. classes in those days, but David would be along too with his 14.2 h.h. ponies, so we were in all the classes. Boxes may have been smaller but we used to tuck them in. There were no partitions or anything, we just herded the horses in.
>
> I thoroughly enjoyed myself and loved my life. The only thing I lived for was my ponies. When I was nearly eleven, I tried one of David's ponies, Chocolate, who won a fantastic class for me at a show at Dymock. He jumped four clears and 5 feet 2 inches. On my eleventh birthday I was given the ride, and Dad always warmed him up for me before each round, because he bucked so much in the collecting ring that I would have fallen off. But it didn't take Chocolate very long to weigh me up, take advantage of me and start running past the fences, so David had him back.

Fred Broome then bought his daughter a novice 13.2 h.h pony called Nutshell which was initially qualified for the Horse of the Year Show at Harringay by David because Liz was too young, although she made her first Horse of the Year Show appearance on this pony as a twelve-year-old.

David rode the bigger ponies until he was sixteen years old and no longer eligible for junior classes. So, when Liz was thirteen, she took over the ride on the ponies he left behind: the famous old pony Ballan Lad, Chocolate and Nutshell – 'Ballan Lad was marvellous, he won classes for all of us, but he and I didn't make the best of partnerships so Mary had him instead.' Fred Broome bought Liz two new ponies, Goodnight, who cost £8 in Newport Market, and Gypsy, who was Irish. With these two Liz had a

Early days. Fred Broome doing up his daughter Liz's girths at a show on her
pony Nutshell.

couple of really good seasons as a fifteen- and sixteen-year-old, her
last years in junior classes. Although Liz did not travel nearly as
much as today's juniors, when she was sixteen she won the Royal,
Three Counties and Welsh Pony Championships on Gypsy who
was later sold at Wembley to Andrew Fielder.

During this time Liz was a pupil at Larkfield Grammar School
in Chepstow and, unlike her daughter Marie, she enjoyed her
schooldays. After O-levels, Mrs Broome hoped Liz would stay on
for her A-levels and then proceed to university. But by July 1960,
when Liz had completed one of the two years' A-level studies, she
suffered disappointing examination results, attributable purely to
her lack of application. She decided she had either to give up the
horses and do much more studying, or leave school to concentrate
on her riding.

Secretly, she gave herself the following summer holidays to make
up her mind which course to take. The two horses she jumped
during that period were Bess, whom she had from David, and
another mare, Ballan Excelsior: 'They gave me sufficient confidence in my first open classes to want to leave school, but

Mother would never have allowed this.'

But fate was on Liz's side. Fortunately, her mother went to the Rome Olympics with David at the same time as the autumn term began. The family's attention was focussed on her brother, who won the individual bronze medal on Sunsalve. Liz seized the opportunity to end her schooldays and faked a note from her mother saying that her daughter had left school to concentrate on horses:

> I knew Father was on my side and would be right behind my decision, but Mother was quite a different obstacle and I didn't look forward to her return. But when she heard she accepted it as she had everything else we did.

Liz was then employed by her father at £2.50 per week, seven days a week, twenty-four hours a day, and loved every minute of it. It was the mare Bess who did most to establish her confidence in senior classes. Bess was not put down until 1982 at the ripe old age of twenty-eight by which time she had had several foals.

In the saddle, Liz possesses much the same qualities as her brother David who won the World Championship in 1970. She is blessed with an impeccable eye for a stride, the same ability to conjure a marvellous rhythmical stride from almost any horse and a clock in her head developed by the thorough tutelage of her father.

But there, in those early days, the similarities ended. David would sleep on in the mornings, snoozing in the horsebox on the showground while his father exercised the horses, whereas Liz was then, as now, a tremendous worker and self-disciplinarian. Another marked difference is that while David excels under the strain of top international competition, Liz, despite her triumphs in the most hallowed show-jumping arenas of the world, gets more satisfaction from bringing on young horses. This is perhaps a legacy from her younger days when she turned new ponies into money winners instead of sitting on expensive proven mounts.

Fred Broome first saw Bess jumping as a three-year-old in Wales carrying a man. He liked her but couldn't buy her. A year later he succeeded. David rode her first and she really could jump:

> As a five-year-old she was brilliant but David probably asked

her too much too soon. The writing was on the wall that she'd jumped too many big fences with him, so Father gave her to me, just to go round the small Welsh shows and some Young Riders' Classes.

David had already put in a considerable amount of work on Bess by the time Liz took over the ride, having jumped her in the Foxhunter final as a four-year-old in 1958 at the last Horse of the Year Show at Harringay, and then won a class on her in 1959 at the Show's first year at its current venue, Wembley. 'It suited David and me very well because he then had Wildfire as well as Sunsalve and so was going to much bigger, more important shows.'

In 1960, Liz won the Young Riders' Championship of Great Britain on Ballan Excelsior at the inaugural meeting of Douglas Bunn's Hickstead, which was a far cry from the great international arena of the eighties. In the same year she made her international debut with Ballan Excelsior at Amsterdam. In 1961 she travelled to Venice Lido, where, riding Gay Monty, she was a member of the winning British team at the Junior European Show Jumping Championships. Her fellow members were the late Douglas Coakes; Michael Cresswell, who now farms in Worcestershire and is married to Alan Oliver's sister Viv; and Jane Kidd, whose main equestrian interest has become dressage.

She began accumulating international jumping experience as an individual at Rotterdam in 1961, and Barcelona in 1962. In 1963 she was a senior team member for the first time at Ostend and Rotterdam. In Belgium the fences, 'were enormous ... it was one great shock for me and turned out to be a massacre'. Matters improved at Rotterdam. Bess jumped two clears in the Nations' Cup and was second in the Grand Prix. That November Liz made her first appearance at Geneva with Bess, and Lirep who was lent to her by a fellow Welsh competitor, Pat Price.

Ted and Liz became engaged on her twenty-first birthday in 1964. They had met on the circuit and known each other for four years.

Liz, aged seventeen, seen here on Bess. She is wearing her first pair of boots, racing ones, obviously made for someone else, because they were kept up by a strap through the button of her breeches.

As a teenager, Liz led a relatively sheltered life, her major contacts with the outside world coming through competing at shows and the Young Farmers' Club. She first met Ted in 1960, when he had sold Discutido to her father and came to deliver the Argentinian horse. Liz recalls that he came with a friend, Graham Aston, whom she thought much the nicer of the two. Thereafter, she continually ran into Ted at shows. They gradually became closer through sharing the same interests and friends, and they started going out together.

When Millie Broome heard that her innocent daughter had been out with the notorious 'Mr Ted' whose wild reputation was enough to horrify any girl's mother, she was not well pleased. But Liz, seventeen at the time and already as decisive as she is now, smiles as she remembers, 'Ted would have married me when I was eighteen, but I had already made a mark in my mind that I would marry him when I was twenty-one years old.' Their wedding took place in November 1964 at Caerwent, not in the local church because it couldn't house all Liz's Scottish and Welsh relations and Ted's wide circle of friends from Warwickshire. Ted and Liz went off to a honeymoon in Majorca, leaving their friends celebrating at the Beaufort Hotel, Tintern, in the Wye Valley. ('How they got home, I'll never know,' says Liz.)

1964 provided a show-jumping as well as a personal milestone when Bess won the Ladies National Championship at the Royal Show which was held on the Great Yorkshire showground at Harrogate.

As his father was ill, Ted was committed to running the family farm. His mare Jane Summers was at the twilight of a long and honourable career so he retired her and gave Liz the ride on Jacapo until the end of the season. Liz took him over at the Bath and West Show. He was an able horse and gave her plenty of fun and success winning both the National Championship at the Royal Show and the Royal International Puissance at White City.

1964 was the year of the Tokyo Olympic Games and, on the strength of these achievements, Liz found herself under serious consideration to represent Great Britain but:

> I didn't feel it was my cup of tea. I never fancied putting that
> sort of pressure on myself. I have always loved doing the job but

Ted and Liz relaxing at home soon after their marriage, at Ponderosa; with them is their Jack Russell, Texas.

not under immense pressure, rather the same as I feel now. I kept Jacapo as long as I dared, right up to Ascot in the middle of August, and then I gave him to David because we were so short of Olympic horses that it was obvious Jacapo would go whoever rode him. I had been told by the selectors that I could go on him but I also felt that it would be criminal if David did not go, so he rode the horse for a month and then took him to Japan.

Partly because David and Liz ride so similarly, Jacapo jumped superbly for David and put up the best performance in the final Olympic trial over an enormous track at the now defunct British Timken Show at Duston, Northampton.

Ted and Liz in a hunter trials competition. Liz recalls, 'He did nothing but advise me all the way round.' (*Same-Day Photos*)

David did not bring home a medal from Tokyo, but Liz is so self-effacing that she would never even consider that Jacapo could have gone better for her after the confidence the combination had gained over the preceding summer. While Jacapo was in Tokyo, Ted sold him to Cynthia Inskip, so on his return the horse went to a new home and the proceeds of the sale went to build the Edgars' bungalow, 'Ponderosa', at Elms Farm, ready for their wedding in November 1964. Later, Alan Oliver rode Jacapo for his new owner.

The problem of whether or not to compete in major competitions has remained an intermittent one for Liz since then: 'The only reason I would compete in a major championship is to try and win.' A similar situation was to arise some two decades later, before the 1982 World Championships at Dublin, when Liz was assured of a team place with Everest Forever but declined to go, thus giving Nick Skelton a chance with Everest If Ever.

In World Championships a different formula is used from other competitions. After the team championship, the four individuals with the best points ride first their own, and then each other's horses, over a comparatively simple course to decide who is World Champion. Liz has reservations about the competition:

> If I were to reach the last four and be faced with the ride on three horses I had never sat on before, at that level, it would quite simply be too much for me even to consider. Feeling like that about the final round, if I reached it, made me decide it would be better not to start.

But by 1983, with vast experience now behind her, Liz would jump willingly if chosen in a European Championship, providing she had a good horse going well enough to have a realistic chance of success. The controversial change horse ride-off is not used in European Championships.

Looking back on her career Liz admits:

> I didn't appreciate nice young horses until I was married and a bit older. I think that goes for all young people – all you want to do at first is get on and jump. When we were kids and Father bought a new pony we were all keen to give it a jump and see who could pinch it first.
>
> I like young horses because every day they make a little improvement. Even if they do only one thing better than they did it yesterday you can be happy because they are progressing. If you go to a show and they jump a clear that's splendid. If they get in the money, it's even better; and the day they win, it's a bonus. If they have four faults you shouldn't worry about it too much – it happened, but probably they jumped something else very well, so you can feel pleased about that.
>
> Winning a good class with a young horse is everything. If you have a Grade A jumper who is noted, perhaps one of the best in the country, and you have four faults, you feel the biggest idiot that ever sat on a horse. I always feel it's definitely my fault on

Schooling Scotch and Soda on the lunge, Liz at Ponderosa. (*Monty*)

such occasions. Everest Forever is such a high-class jumper that he wouldn't have made the mistake on his own. All your connections are disappointed and, to make matters worse, there is probably at least £100 down the drain.

The number of classes such a horse wins is nearly always decidedly less than the number he starts in and those are the only days everyone is pleased. You can lose out personally with your best horse, but with your youngster you can be happy about something every day.

After Everest Forever won the Aachen Grand Prix from Europe's best in 1980, it was generally assumed that Liz was all set for the

San Antone was a very athletic horse who won Liz many classes. Here he is throwing an unorthodox but very effective jump on the sacred turf of the Wembley Stadium. (*Monty*)

Substitute Olympic Games in Rotterdam, but the idea did not appeal to her. She had never fancied the original venue of Moscow and thought, 'What's the point in using up my horse when I shan't even be getting the thrills of the actual contest?'

In any event, Liz never had to make a final decision because about six weeks before the competition, Forever picked up a virus. His form dipped quickly, his condition deteriorated and he could not have survived the big testing courses in such low physical shape.

Since their marriage Ted has provided Liz with a constant stream of horses. Of the many she has tried, the chestnut San Antone stands out as one of the nicest and most capable. Ted

FACING PAGE
Liz and Forever head the line-up after winning the BSJA Ladies National Championship at Royal Windsor in 1982. (*Bob Langrish*)

bought him in 1966 whereupon Liz began jumping him in novice classes and he proved a real winner, taking many competitions. He was brilliant against the clock, had all the ability in the world and was very careful. His one failing was water which he would not jump, so he excelled indoors where water jumps are rare.

In 1969 Liz and Ted travelled to Hamburg with San Antone and Uncle Max whom Ted had bought the previous year. Liz won the Ladies Class and rode in the Derby. In 1970 San Antone was sold to a young Warwickshire rider, Carol Turvey.

When they came home from Germany, Ted bought the dun Timmie whom Liz jumped throughout 1970. The arrival of Maria, Ted and Liz's only child, in February 1971, barely interfered with Liz's riding. She had last ridden Timmie at Amsterdam in November 1970, and was back in action with him at Taplow Show on Easter Monday, 1971.

Liz looked after Marie, as she is now known because she prefers the name to Maria, for the first two months of her daughter's life:

> Then I decided this was not really my job, and it was interfering with my horses. I asked a friend of mine, Nicky (known to all as the 'Gorgeous Groom'), who was working for the local vet, to come and look after Marie, but at first she refused, saying she knew nothing about small children. I told her that I didn't know much either but I had survived, so I persuaded her to join us. Nicky was an excellent nanny and enjoyed looking after Marie, as well as life with us and the horses. Altogether, she stayed for two and a half years.

1971 also saw the purchase of Makedo, whose position as Liz's favourite-ever horse is unlikely to be surpassed:

> Ted saw him jumping at the Horse of the Year Show at Wembley, loved what he saw, and was able to buy him from John Lanni. He was difficult to get on with and it was not until the end of 1972 that I found the key and was able to ride him properly. From then on he was fantastic.

Not a top international in scope, Makedo was considerably better than a speed horse, and in 1973 won many jump-off classes as well

Makedo, Liz's favourite friend, winning a class for her at the Royal Winter Fair
at Toronto in 1977.

as those straight against the clock. The Usher Vaux Gold Tankard
at the Royal Highland is a competition that all the riders want to
win so they start their best horses. In 1974, Makedo delighted Liz
by out-jumping them all:

I was so proud of him that day. With his lesser ability it was
harder for him to win that than for Forever to win the Aachen
Grand Prix. He tried so hard that, from the saddle, his little feet
were coming out of his earholes.

In the autumn Makedo travelled with the British team to Laxenburg near Vienna and, in the park surrounding one of the Haps-
burgs' summer palaces where the tragic Elizabeth Empress of
Austria used to find solace riding her horses, achieved two clears
in the Nations' Cup. Liz was rewarded with two gold coins weighing an ounce each with which she will never part. Her special
affection for Makedo developed because he was not easy and at a
time when he was her only open horse, used to 'fill all the spaces,
jumping all the big classes, and some speed too'.

When Makedo came to Leek Wootton, although he was promising, it was not apparent that he would ever attain such an esteemed
position in his rider's heart. He was very uninteresting, thin, had
a vice in that he was a windsucker, and was nervy both in and out
of the stable. 'When I rode him, the more mistakes I made, the
more nervy he became.' There was a great deal to overcome, and
the girl who had just come to work for Liz in his second season,
Fenella Power ('Hob'), really took to him and looked after him
very quietly.

> Gradually Hob's special care, combined with my trying to ride
> him properly, totally changed him. It took two years and he
> altered from a nervous little horse to a pet. He died after an
> operation following severe colic in June 1982, when he was
> eighteen years old.

The great Irish horse Boomerang who was later to carry Eddie
Macken to a remarkable sequence of four consecutive Hickstead
Derby victories arrived in May 1972. Ted had bought him from
the yard of the former European Ladies Champion, Iris Kellett,
near Dublin. He had been sent there to be sold at the Dublin
Spring Show where he was third in a novice class. Ironically, it was
Eddie Macken, who worked for Iris Kellett at the time and later
partnered Boomerang in many great triumphs, who rode him for
Ted to see the day he bought him.

By Battleburn, out of a hunter mare, the five-year-old had
already been hunted for two seasons. Ted bought him specifically
for Liz. She found Boomerang

> a dream of a novice. He had more seconds than firsts because I

didn't pull him around against the clock. He didn't have the best mouth so I tended to let him go in his own way but he never had fences down, he just jumped clear after clear after clear.

During his attempt to qualify for the Foxhunter Championship, Boomerang picked up a touch of pneumonia shortly before his regional final at the Staffordshire County Show. The vet gave him the all clear just before and although Liz took him straight from the stable, he lacked work and jumped very high over all the jumps. Unhappily they included water which proved his undoing, so illustrating the element of luck essential in show-jumping, because during the seventies, Boomerang became one of the world's best horses.

It was a big disappointment, but after that, in October, he won the Dick Turpin Stakes at the Horse of the Year Show. Then in 1973 Liz took him to Amsterdam where he won a class and also to Geneva with the British team. Boomerang's potential was now clear for all to see and all that year the Edgars were plagued with offers. Eventually he was sold to Leon Melchior. It broke Liz's heart to see him go, but the horse had already had some problems with his feet and the Edgars were uncertain how long he would remain one hundred per cent sound. By the time Boomerang was in his prime, and seldom beaten all over the world in partnership with Eddie Macken, he had been de-nerved. Like most international show-jumpers Liz and Ted know more now than they did about keeping horses sound, and, at the time, they were surprised he continued to jump so well for so long. If they had him now they would not sell him. 'Another reason was that Ted thought I'd never do what Eddie could do with him, and he was quite right, but if Nick had been around it could have been a different story.'

Melchior, a Dutch multi-millionaire, rode Boomerang himself and when Ted saw them compete at Lucerne the following year Boomerang wouldn't even jump the first fence. Ted tried to buy the horse back, but to no avail. Eventually Paul Schockemohle bought him as a speed horse for himself. At that time Eddie was working for Paul, which was how he came to ride Boomerang. Then he was bought by German owner Doctor Schnapka, who owned the Ferrins Stud in Ireland, and when Eddie returned home Boomerang went too.

At about the same time Liz was bringing on the novice Wallaby who, although not her favourite, proved a marvellous horse. When Ted sold Boomerang in 1973 and was looking for a replacement in Germany, he found Wallaby in soon to be World Champion Hartwig Steenken's stables where he'd been for little over a month. As Wallaby walked down the ramp, Liz couldn't believe her eyes. 'He was the same colour, the same model, the same markings, everything the same as Boomerang. I took him into the school and jumped him loose and it was incredible, he also had the same jump.'

He seemed too good to be true. Liz took him to a little show at Hilton Park near Wolverhampton on a Wednesday night, wearing Boomerang's bridle and Boomerang's rugs.

I thought he was a special horse but we got eliminated at the second fence which was about three feet high. I came out and Ted was so disappointed that he got on himself, gave him a school, went in the next class and was eliminated, at the third fence. Wallaby had an 'Oh be joyful' squaring up over the next two days at home and by the time I took him back to Hilton Park the following Sunday, he jumped two clears and was third in a huge Foxhunter Class.

Wallaby had revealed his true colours and from then on Liz reckoned Ted was responsible for all his wins. Ted did all the work on the horse, rode him at home and kept him straight. The horse developed into a big winner and in 1977 raised the Union Jack in front of an 18,000 crowd under the glittering lights of Madison Square Garden, when he carried Liz to become the first English rider to capture the Grand Prix of New York since Harvey Smith in 1967.

That win had involved an early start for Ted, who had been up at the allotted time of five o'clock that morning, sharpening up Wallaby in the limited collecting-ring space before the horse's brief exercise time in the arena an hour later.

To this day, Wallaby, who was fourteen in 1983, is most often ridden by Nick and will duck out if he can. Says Liz, 'He's a naughty boy but a lovable devil, well worth persevering with because he is an out and out jumper, a quality possessed by few horses.' Despite his faults, in June 1977 he won Liz her first National Amateur Championship at Cardiff, and then, the following month, her first Queen Elizabeth II Cup at the Royal International Horse Show. With the demise of the World and European Ladies Championships, this is now the premier contest restricted solely to lady riders.

Everest Mayday who was previously ridden by Mallowry Spens won Liz her second National Ladies Championship in 1975 and also provided her with the occasional 'scarey' ride because she could never be sure she could hold him. Another problem was that she could not guarantee she would be in the place she wanted to be on take-off for a fence because he had totally different ideas:

> He was very fast and very careful and quite a special little horse. If we'd have had him now, Nick would have ridden him and I think he'd have won even more classes. I don't often remember exact details of classes I've won, but I can remember all of those on Mayday because of sheer excitement or fright.

In December 1976, Ted went to Germany to see some horses at Axel Wockener's yard and Leicestershire international Tim Grubb, who is now married to United States International showjumper Michele McEvoy, travelled with him. Although Ted was unaware at the time, this was to prove a momentous journey, for Ted was to purchase that much sought and most elusive of equines, a world class show-jumper – Forever. This was the horse who would later give Liz the enthusiasm to continue jumping internationally and take her to the very top when, otherwise, she could well have elected to concentrate on her first love, bringing on novices to the national scene.

Tim suggested to Ted that he ask Axel to show him the young horse which he had seen jumping several months ago and which he described as 'exceptional'. Axel didn't want to show Ted the horse because he had a wind problem and six weeks previously he'd had a second operation. Even when pressed Axel refused to bring the horse out of the stable. Eventually, he put a price on the horse which Ted agreed in the stable without even seeing him led out!

Ted said, 'He's my horse, I own him now, so I'd like to see him

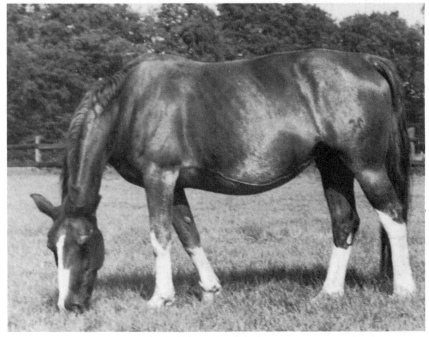

Pedigree of a champion. Forever was foaled at Dingstede near Oldenburg on 23rd April 1972. His head is remarkably like that of his dam, Dietrich Schütte's Dulderliese (BELOW LEFT). Her sire, Düppel comes from one of the best Hanoverian lines, while one of her maternal great-grandsires, Almfreund, is highly regarded in Germany.

Futuro (ABOVE LEFT – photo *Werner Ernst*) has an interesting combination of French blood through his Normandy dam Fabienne, and sire, Furioso, considered one of the world's best show-jumping stallions, having sired d'Oriola's Lutteur B and Pomone.

Forever's staying power is inherited through Furioso whose sire Precipitation and grandsire Hurry On are descendants of the famous Matchem line. Precipitation was a stayer, won the Ascot Gold Cup and sired the Derby and St Leger winner Airborne.

Forever's size – he stands 17 hands high – can be traced back to Jockey Club Cup winner Hurry On. A magnificent chestnut, he was massive for a stayer and sired three Derby winners: Coronach, Captain Cuttle and Call Boy.

OPPOSITE Forever and Liz at the Royal International Horse Show in 1982. A good example of a horse bringing his forearms up. (*Kit Houghton*)

JAN 13ᵗ 1977

♔ OLDENBURG

Forever

Der Züchter Dietr. Schütte - Dingstede   Kreis: Oldenburg

hat nachstehende Stute decken lassen.

Name und Nr.: Dulderliese 84595	bedeckt von Hengst: Futuro 4352 am: 9.5.1971
Geb.-Jahr: 1965 Farbe und Abz.: F.,	am:
schiefe bis in d.r.NÜ.r.Bls.,Utl.w., bd.Vo.u.Hf.h.w.	am:

Aus vorstehender Bedeckung ist nachfolgendes Fohlen gefallen: Geschlecht: H e n g s t   geb. am: 23.4.1972

Farbe und Abzeichen: F., Bls.in l.NÜ.r.,Utl.w., bd.Vf.u.r.Hf.h.w.

Eigentümer der Stute z. Z. des Abfohlens: Dietr. Schütte - Dingstede

Fohlenbrand (linker Hinterschenkel)

Vater:			
	Furioso xx	Precipitation	Hurry on
			Double Life
Futuro 4352		Laureen	Son in Law
			St. Prisca
	Fabienne (Norm.)	Hedjaz ou Vert Galant	Ulon
			Vaillante
		Rigolette	Vingt Mai
			Hongue

Mutter:			
	Düppel 3955 (Hann.)	Bömitz I 2574	Dollart 3253
			*Clepp H 28573
Dulderliese 84595		*Amtsjägerin H 59208	Abendsport 3109
			Abeduta H 34901
	*Eichdirndl H 60509	Elimar 3762	Almfreund I 3242
			*Flürenne H 35513
		Feindgüttin H 54414	Feindflug 3311
			*Florlie H 44385

Stutbucheintragung:

in das _____

eingetragen

Name: _____ Nr.: _____
_____ , den _____
i. A.

Stutbuchführer

HDP. Eintragung (für Turnierpferde)

Name: Forever

Bes.: _____

ist unter Nr. _____

in die Liste _____ für inländische Warmblut-
pferde des Hauptverbandes für Zucht und
Prüfung deutscher Pferde eingetragen.

_____ , den _____
i. A.

* = staatl. prämiiert

29 Oldenburg, den 15. Juli 1972   und   weitere Generationen (siehe Rückseite)

49733

Stutbuchführer

trot out and pop a pole.' They took him out, put up a little pole and he soared over with a huge, beautifully rounded bascule. 'Once was enough, he was all I'd hoped.'

When she first saw this prospective superstar on January 13th, 1977, Liz's first impression was: 'Awful. He was a big, raw-boned, ewe-necked thing, extremely travel-sick, unhappy, and looked a real mess.' The Edgars decided that when Forever came to England they would not ask him to do anything at all for at least six weeks, but because he looked so bad Ted thought Liz should see him jump. They took him to the school, where he trotted round and went six feet high in the air over a three-feet pole.

'Just for that one jump he was already a king in our stables,' Liz reminisces. From that moment on Forever had the best stable, the best rugs, the best bandages and the best treatment.

The horse could not be worked because of the recent operation and this proved an advantage. Forever was long-reined and ridden in the school, but no faster than at the walk. Liz wonders now if this initial enforced restraint is why the horse is so polite, mannerly and pleasant in his outlook. It was over a month before he gradually progressed from a walk to a slow trot. He wasn't pushed or forced. There was no temptation to put him into the ring a week after they had him and meanwhile the horse did everything right. In April when he had learnt to canter correctly round the school, Liz was tempted to take him to a small show at the British Equestrian Centre at Stoneleigh and he jumped three clear rounds in his first-ever competition in a Newcomers' Qualifier.

1977 was taken at a gentle pace and after competing at three small indoor shows Liz took him to the Wales and West Show where 'it was like sitting on dynamite. It was a bit windy and Forever exploded round the little ring, but he did all I asked and took to jumping like a duck to water.'

Forever won the Grafton Hunt Show Foxhunter Class which qualified him for his Regional Final which was the only time he had a course which suited him. He was always likely to be beaten against the clock because Liz refused to rush him on account of his size. 'I never jumped him on bad ground, and never in the rain because I don't like it and I didn't think it would do him any good either.' If Liz arrived at a show where the ground was rough or hard she took him home without competing. He did all he was asked perfectly the first time, it was just a matter of patiently waiting for him to grow up.

On a trip to Malcolm Bowey's permanent arena at Stannington, Northumberland, which is now closed, he learnt to jump water and ditches, slipping over effortlessly the first time he faced them.

At Stoneleigh, Forever qualified for the Elizabeth Ann Grade C Championship and also reached the Foxhunter final. In the Elizabeth Ann final, Forever was second to John Brown's lovely bay mare Our Gaytime, and then following in the steps of Boomerang, another great horse failed to win the Foxhunter when a brick fell off the wall.

All the experts who had seen Forever jump knew he was outstanding; but as Liz took him home for his winter's rest it was the words of Harvey Smith ('who is never one to bullshit', says Liz) that kept ringing in her ears: 'By gum, he's a sweet one for a German, isn't he?'

In April 1978 he made his debut as a Grade B horse at Hickstead, which was later to become the scene of some of his greatest triumphs, and on consecutive days he won all three Futurity Classes which are specially designed by Douglas Bunn to bring on promising international-type horses.

Forever's next milestone was down in the Mendip Hills at the Royal Bath and West Show at Shepton Mallet, a notable venue where the top riders compete whenever possible. Liz won an important class on Wallaby but got tremendous satisfaction from the fact that Forever jumped the big course well to finish third. The rest of the week he was not 'asked', just 'fiddled', round in small classes, and then continued to 'fiddle' at mostly small shows for the rest of the season.

Basically he filled the role of Makedo's back-up horse, more often than not going to largely minor shows. But all the time he was being made, jumping in proper classes with a jump-off. This is a less lucrative proposition than speed classes at big shows but is the best way to develop a show-jumper.

In July at Northampton, he was started in a bigger more important competition, the AIT where his win provided another notch in his belt and qualified him for the Queen Elizabeth II Cup the following year.

All summer, Liz had harboured a growing ambition to win the

Sanyo Talent Spotters' Championship at the Stoneleigh Autumn Show in late October, to atone for Forever's Foxhunter failure.

At the Dublin Indoor Show he achieved his first international victory, taking the big jump-off class. In 1977, Liz had toyed with the idea of taking Forever as second horse to the States to back Wallaby but decided against it because she knew the horse would have attracted an offer of such magnitude it would be difficult to refuse and this win vindicated her decision.

In 1979 Forever found his form at Whitsuntide but kept 'having a fence down and playing around'. Liz thought he was 'taking the mickey' out of her. On the second day at the South of England at Ardingly, Sussex he stopped and received the first whack of his life in the ring. He was so surprised that he jumped the fence and came out the next day to be second in the AIT, then travelled the next week to Cardiff where he won Liz her second Amateur Championship. Wins followed in quick succession, two at the Royal Highland near Edinburgh, one at the Royal at Stoneleigh and then he carried Liz to her second Queen's Cup triumph at the Royal International.

On the strength of these results, Liz was selected to ride with the British team for Forever's first CSIO at Hickstead but was never likely to jump in the team as it was the time when the great quartet of David Broome, the late Caroline Bradley, Derek Ricketts and Malcolm Pyrah all had top-class horses. This foursome were next to win the European Championship at Rotterdam.

Forever won a £1,000 class on the first day and was third in the Grand Prix, which was headed by Robert Smith on Video, a great performance for a seven-year-old in this class of competition.

The Queen's and King's Cup winners are almost always selected for Dublin and Liz duly found herself there, but it was not a notable experience because it was very wet and the deep, heavy going was not ideal for Forever. Back home his confidence was soon restored at some small shows.

Forever kicked off in 1980 by winning the AIT at Badminton Horse Trials and progressed to take the May Hickstead Grand Prix and then the Aachen Grand Prix which is one of the world's most difficult and coveted classes. No toughie – despite her realistic approach to the sport – even Liz shed a sentimental tear, along with 45,000 Germans, as she led the parade for the traditional emotive Aachener farewell, the Abschied der Nationen. At this ceremony those present create a man-made snow-storm by waving goodbye with clean white handkerchieves bought especially for the occasion, to the tune of an old German folksong, best known as the late Elvis Presley's hit, 'Wooden Heart'.

Almost immediately after Aachen came the Royal – on the Edgars' doorstep at the National Agricultural Centre three miles away. Here, Forever won Liz the caravan that was awarded to the show's leading rider.

Forever then travelled north up the M6 to Arena North, near Charnock Richard in Lancashire (no longer a going concern because of economic reasons), and, in the spectacular sunken amphitheatre, captured the last Bass Charrington Grand National.

This glorious run of success now came to a temporary halt. Forever's form started to go downhill when he went to the Royal International in July 1980 and was second in the Queen's Cup to Caroline Bradley and Tigre. 'He found it very hard work and was like a dead duck to ride. I only kept him going because I was under pressure in view of the approaching Substitute Olympics, but there was no doubt that he was lifeless and not at all himself.' Although Forever won a few other classes, one at the Sanyo Autumn Championships at Stoneleigh, he was never right again in 1980 nor one hundred per cent throughout 1981.

When a consistent horse loses his form there is generally a reason. Tests on Forever's blood showed that he had picked up a virus.

His first 1981 show was the Birmingham Indoor International in April. Forever's coat looked terrible, he was dull and listless, had no jump and stopped on the first day at the first fence. Liz was sure he was still affected by the virus and took him straight home. Liz and Ted tried all they knew to regain his condition and form but it was not until Suffolk County in June that Forever's coat shone, a sure sign of well-being. At last he won a class.

Once he began to improve, he was picked for the Paris International where he was fourth in the Grand Prix. Travelling on to Aachen both Forever and Malcolm Pyrah's Towerlands Anglezarke achieved double clears in the Nations' Cup team which finished first in a big ten-team line-up and secured the first British victory since 1967. By now he was going well but still lacked spark.

At the Royal International he won Liz her third Queen Elizabeth II Cup from Caroline Bradley on Trimoco Manuel, and helped provide a rewarding occasion for Everest Double Glazing by finishing second to Nick Skelton on St James in the Everest Grand Prix on the final night.

Along with her brother David (Mr Ross), Malcolm Pyrah (Towerlands Anglezarke) and John Whitaker (Ryan's Son), Liz was chosen for the European Championships, which were held in the 1972 Olympic Equestrian Stadium at Riem, near Munich. She decided to travel there slowly in late August and compete on the way to keep an edge on Forever. The horse was fourth in the St Gallen Grand Prix in Switzerland, and then, in the Donaueschingen Grand Prix, second to the great combination of Austrian Hugo Simon and Gladstone who had won the Substitute Olympic Games individual gold medal the previous year.

It had been an encouraging warm-up for Munich, especially when Liz could not have envisaged competing there as recently as three months earlier. She found that

> Forever still did not feel as good as he had the year before and therefore not as able to help me out of any awkward situation I might get him into, but I make no excuses for Munich. I blame myself because I made a mistake on the second day of the team competition at the combination. I found myself committed on far too long a stride so Forever missed the first element, it went down and he stopped at the second, so I had seven faults. The next time he jumped it perfectly. Then I hurried like mad to avoid time faults and had another fence down. It was a disastrous round of eleven faults plus some time faults.

Forever jumped clear on the third day but it was all over. In top international competition such errors prove costly, one bad round is one too many. Germany won the team competition from Switzerland and Holland, and Britain was fourth: 'Fortunately Malcolm

HRH Princess Anne presents Liz with the Queen Elizabeth II Cup which she won on Forever at the Royal International Horse Show in July, 1981. (*Findlay Davidson*)

was a real star and took the individual silver medal just behind Paul Schockemohle on Deister, who has never gone better, so nobody noticed what had happened to me.'

Forever then went to Calgary (Canada) with the British team that was beaten by Holland by one time fault, jumped at the Horse of the Year Show without much success, won the Grand Prix at the Dublin Indoor International in November, and in December was second in the Paris World Cup Qualifier to Switzerland's Willi Melliger on Trumpf Burr.

His final outing for 1981 was at Olympia where he is never at his best although he nearly won a class which fell to Nick on St James, but 'nearly is not good enough'. Forever's 1981 record commands respect, but for a horse that was firmly established amongst the world's top Grand Prix horses, it was apparent that he could not have been one hundred per cent physically fit for much of the time.

1982 opened with a few small shows, then the Birmingham Indoor International, and in April, the World Cup final in Gothenburg, where Forever finished sixth overall behind United States rider Melanie Smith on Calypso. The Americans have a fine record in this contest having won four of the five contests, including the fifth running at Vienna in April 1983 when Norman Dello Joio won on the French-bred stallion I Love You.

In 1982 British hopes for Gothenburg were reduced because the horses suffered a desperately bad sea crossing, involving a twenty-four-hour journey from Harwich. They were all very travel-sick on arrival after a terribly rough passage which took the stuffing right out of them. Forever was not even jumped on the first trial day.

After his see-saw form of 1981, in 1982 Forever was infinitely more consistent and at the Royal Windsor Horse Show in May, won Liz her fourth Ladies National Championship. He then

While Ted was away looking at horses in Australia, Liz took advantage of the occasion to enjoy a day's sport on his star hunter Grandpa. The occasion was a joint invitation meet of the North Warwickshire and Curre, of which David Broome is a Joint Master. Here in front of Mr and the Hon. Mrs Charles Smith–Ryland's Sherbourne Park are Liz and David. (*Ann Martin*)

jumped with the British team in Lucerne where Britain won the Nations' Cup. Pam Dunning was the architect of this victory with two superb clears on her brave little New Zealand horse Roscoe, who was so tragically to break a leg jumping at Hickstead on his return home. Says Liz, 'Although we won the Nations' Cup, it was due to Roscoe who coped best with the disastrously heavy ground. It was not that we were so good but that the rest were worse.'

At Aachen Forever jumped two clears in the Nations' Cup which was won by Germany. Britain was second. Forever had by now established a remarkable Queen Elizabeth II Cup record having won in 1979 and 1981 and been second in 1980. In July at Wembley he won the trophy a third time. In the Donaueschingen Grand Prix, Forever managed to reverse the previous year's result, triumphing and relegating Hugo Simon on Gladstone to second place.

At the Horse of the Year Show he won the Griffin and Brand Cup. Liz then decided he had done enough and needed a full winter's rest so he was turned out with Wallaby.

Forever was out at grass by day and by night. Throughout this period his grazing was well supplemented with two substantial feeds a day of oats, a few nuts and chaff which were increased if there was a hard white frost or if the weather was really cold or wet.

Eleven years old in 1983, Forever possesses all the qualities necessary to equip a jumper to face the courses of the eighties. He has the ideal temperament and jumps because he enjoys it:

I've never needed any assistance or anyone to bully him into jumping, he does what I ask and is the perfect gentleman. One contributory factor is that he has so much innate ability that he has found he can easily do everything asked of him.

However, in his box, this paragon can be a demon when he gets fit:

When he first arrived he cornered his groom by the manger and wouldn't let her out on more than one occasion. One day he did something to Nick in the stable and Nick came out raging. He was going to give him a walloping but Ted told him to leave the horse alone because Forever's great-grandsire was Precipitation, who was noted for being a very difficult stallion, especially in his stable. Ted advised that we should all treat Forever with respect, making sure we didn't get bitten or kicked and so avoid a confrontation.

Forever could be very cute. Sometimes he'd pick up a back leg and as you moved forward to miss it, he'd bite you, or he would flash his teeth and as you shot backwards out of the way, he'd kick you. He had the situation totally weighed up and, even to this day, you can't guarantee you won't be kicked or bitten changing his rugs if he's not tied up! Nevertheless he's a lovable horse and full of character.

In January 1981, because of the continuing controversy about professionalism and the names of the sponsored horses, Liz turned professional. The BSJA had introduced a rule that only professionals could ride a horse with a sponsor's prefix. Liz explains:

As we were well established with Everest Double Glazing and they had always been so good to us, the only way to have the Everest prefix on the name Forever, and any of the other horses I ride, was to turn professional. Nevertheless, apart from riding horses carrying our sponsor's name, I think I'm just about the staunchest amateur in the game. I only ride when I have time, I keep house, look after Marie and Ted, and am probably the least professional of the professionals.

CHAPTER THREE

NICK SKELTON

'If,' Liz is wont to say, 'Ted could order a son, it would be Nick.'
They first heard of Nick in the summer of 1973 through Ted's
life-long friend Lol Weaver. He mentioned one day that a friend
of his had a lad who needed some help with his jumping as his
pony wasn't going too well. Could he bring it over?

Predictably, the answer was yes, and when the lad duly arrived
with the pony, only Liz was at home. She gave the pony a jump
and tried to help Nick. That evening Ted returned and asked her
what the pony had been like. Liz, who has the same flair for
detecting embryo talent that Ted demonstrates in his purchases of
novice horses (like a ferret in search of a rabbit), replied, 'The pony
was useless, but I think the kid is brilliant. He reminded me of my
brother in the old days. There was something I had to like, he had
so much natural ability.'

Nick remembers:

I was fifteen at the time, and had only one thought in my mind:
to be a National Hunt jockey. Although I jumped my pony and
came over that once to Liz, to try and get my pony going,
show-jumping did not really appeal to me. I was interested and
enjoyed it, but not as a career – I was going to be a National
Hunt jockey.

Whenever there was racing on telly, I'd watch it, and then I'd
go out and practise on my pony with my knees up round my
ears. I built myself some fences and away I went at the gallop,
all day long, round and round the field. I just loved it.

Heeding Liz's comments about Nick, Ted asked Nick's father,
David Skelton, if his son would like to try jumping at the Edgar
yard during the first summer he left school before he went racing,

offering a couple of novices for the lad to ride.

At first Nick did not want to go but his father changed his mind by pointing out that only the top two or so National Hunt jockeys really made any money out of the sport. Once Nick had a taste of the jumping game proper, he never wanted to leave.

The two novices Nick rode for Ted and Liz that first summer 'weren't even decent. We used to have some rough horses compared to those we have now. Those were the poor days, the "ride anything" days.' The first horse he had for Ted at home was the dun, Timmie, who had already won many classes for Liz and was later sold on to Ann Davies. It was this old, experienced horse who convinced Nick he wanted to show-jump rather than race ride as a career. Then he had The Red Baron who Johnnie Fahey had brought over from Australia.

Resolve and determination can already be seen in Nick's jaw. He is seated sixth from the left on his pony.

The first novice Nick rode was called Hello: 'He was at least eighteen hands high, probably 18.6! A really big horse, I didn't get on very well with him at all.'

On Friday, April 5th, 1974, Nick left school. His father David received a letter from the headmaster of Bablake School, Coventry, which read: 'We think it would be better if your son did not continue his education at this school because his outdoor activities are obviously more important to him.' The headmaster was of course correct and Nick immediately went to ride full-time for Ted and Liz.

One of the first shows he went to was Amberley with Hello:

I shan't forget that day. I was jumping a fence away from the collecting ring, Hello hit it and we both somersaulted onto the ground. He rolled all over me and I was really crushed, somehow I struggled up and I remember laughing about it then with Liz.

Other novices at this time were Esquire, and Maybe, who holds the exalted position of being Nick's most special horse. Liz, who had ridden Maybe as a novice, told Nick he napped really badly. At mid-day one Sunday, Ted, dressed up in a smart suit and going out for the day, noticed Liz having trouble with Maybe a couple of fields away. He went over and jumped on saying, 'I'll get him going.' He stayed in the field until four o'clock in the afternoon and still Maybe wouldn't move forwards, backwards or sideways.

It was another day before Maybe was persuaded to see the error of his ways and proceed forward.

Maybe was bought from Freddy Cottam who rode him to win several Foxhunter competitions but considered his character somewhat difficult. Gradually he has mellowed with age. In July, Nick had his first taste of international competition when he was picked to ride in the Junior European Championships at Lucerne in Switzerland along with four girls: Debbie Johnsey, Vicky Turner, Lynn Chapman and Cheryl Walker. Britain finished second in the Nations' Cup and Maybe had a clear and four faults.

At the Horse of the Year Show at Wembley that October, spectators saw a rising star when Nick won the Whitbread Young Riders' Competition on Maybe. Nick felt sure he'd made the right decision about his future.

Two contented show-jumpers. Nick relaxing on his favourite partner, Maybe. (Ian Tyas, *Keystone Press*)

At this time, Maybe was still inclined to nap on occasion and the previous summer at the Shrewsbury Flower Show, he'd refused to go at the start although it was towards home. Nick was forced to get off and lead him and he had to do this more than once.

He'll always be my favourite horse because he was the first good one I ever had and I grew up with him. Although he was a little demon to start with, he set me on my way, winning all the junior championships there were. Then, in 1978, he went on to win for me the Basildon Bond Championship for the Leading Show Jumper of the Year, when it was still a three-round rather than a two-round class and tougher than it is now. Two years later he carried me to a team silver medal at the Substitute Olympic Games at Rotterdam in 1980. Ted would tell you he'd kick in the stable but he wouldn't ... well, not me ... but he'd probably kick Ted. He's as good as gold in the stable.

In 1975 Nick travelled with Ted to the Dublin Spring Show to ride in the British junior team. His horse was the black Himself, who was fifth in the Grand Prix and sold whilst there to Paul Schockemohle and Eddie Macken when they were jumping together and the latter was based in Germany.

Nick recalls that Dublin trip:

Tinka Taylor was our chef d'équipe and this time it was an all-male team, with Gary Widdowson, John Brown and Pip Nichols

who had bought Timmie. 'Right, I want you all in bed early,'
Tinka said the night before the Nations' Cup. We slipped out
through a window, went down the fire escape and made it to a
pub, the Horse Show House, just down the road. We were all
only fifteen or sixteen years old and took advantage of the Irish
hospitality. Tinka caught us merrily walking back into the hotel
through the foyer. She gave us a right stripping off and said she
wanted to see us all in her room at nine the next morning. 'Gang
bang,' someone said and even Tinka had to laugh. I've always
liked her, she's one of the best. Sometimes now she teases me,
'I think you ought to come and keep my juniors in order!'

Nick was really put out in 1975 when Ted told him someone
wanted to buy Maybe. 'I didn't know who it was at first but
naturally didn't like anyone who wanted to have my best horse.'
The would-be buyer was Sir Hugh Fraser, then of Harrods, who
wanted Maybe for himself. His wife Aileen tried Maybe at the
Royal on 2nd July. The following week at the Great Yorkshire
Maybe changed hands. Nick, who was very annoyed, had a word
in Maybe's ear before he went: 'If you'll just revert to your old
tricks, you'll come home.' 'Don't worry,' Ted consoled, 'he'll be
back.' To Nick's joy Maybe must have listened; he repeated his
Shrewsbury misbehaviour up in Scotland, refusing to go through
the start, and was duly collected from Sir Hugh at the East of
England Show the following week and brought back to Leek
Wootton.
    The same year Ted bought OK and showed him to Liz and Nick
in the indoor school when he arrived at Leek Wootton. He had
been bought through Belgian François Mathy, one of the world's
most successful show-jumping dealers, out of a riding school. 'OK
had a hogged mane, he was big, really poor and you could count
all his ribs.' Ted jumped him loose and he was very impressive.
Nick had him to ride, but he was never the most careful horse and
always had to be held together very tightly.
    Nick's first venture abroad with OK was to Lyons, France, in
July where Britain won the Junior Nations' Cup. The Junior
European Championships were in August and Nick was picked to
go on Maybe. But Ted told the selectors that Maybe could not go

Nick winning the European Junior Show Jumping Championship in August 1975 on OK at Dornbirn, Austria. (*Findlay Davidson*)

because of the fact he just might not start; he suggested OK as a substitute and OK duly carried Nick to the 1975 Junior European title.

'It was one of my toughest wins because OK was happy enough to get to the other side but so naturally clumsy he didn't care how he got there.' In retrospect, Nick rode brilliantly because OK was not quite the calibre horse to win the title.

Maybe went lame in September so could not be jumped at the Horse of the Year Show. Nick went with some other horses but it proved a lean week.

In September 1976, Nick was picked for his first CSIO at Laxenburg near Vienna with Maybe and OK but never made the journey because the British team's visit was abandoned at the last minute, the result of a cross-Channel sea-strike. So it was not until 1977 that Nick went to his first senior indoor show, which was Antwerp. Maybe and OK actually arrived this time and Ted took Amigo and Louisiana. Nick did not hit the highlights, but all the time he was acquiring one of the most vital elements of success, experience.

The same year, 1977, Nick finally made his first CSIO in Rotterdam. There was an enormous contingent of Britons: Ann Fenwick, Harvey Smith, Ray Howe, Malcolm Pyrah, Caroline Bradley, Michael Whitaker, Geoff Glazzard with Pennwood Forge Mill, and Ted with Amigo.

In such company, Nick was hardly surprised not to be selected for the Nations' Cup. He took Louisiana and Highland Laddie. Ted travelled Amigo, and Maybe as a speed horse.

The event Nick remembers best was a calamitous three-horse rescue-relay where one rider was meant to be at the central box all the time. In an hilarious round everything went wrong. At one stage, Ted, Ray Howe and Nick were erroneously all out together galloping round the course which they took an incredibly long five minutes to complete.

At the Royal Agricultural Show in 1978, disaster struck. Ted broke his knee in a fall from the grey Lastic and while he was hospitalised had his horses turned out in the field.

The Town and Country Show at Stoneleigh followed soon afterwards and Ted suggested to Liz that Lastic should be got up for Nick to ride.

The new combination went well and Nick then continued to jump Lastic. That autumn Nick finally rode in his first Nations' Cup, at Laxenburg, which he had failed to reach the previous year.

The Laxenburg team, which finished second to Switzerland, was completed by John Brown, David Bowen and Ann Smith. Nick rode Lastic and had two four-fault rounds, both penalties incurred at the first fence.

The phenomenon called 'Skelly' by his friends and rivals alike, was now moving into gear. Taking Lastic and Maybe to the inaugural Dublin Indoor Show, he won the first of a legion of leading rider awards. He had not merely beaten the small fry because the big guns – Harvey Smith, Derek Ricketts, David

Broome, Graham Fletcher and Eddie Macken – were all among the competitors.

At this time Nick, who was 'shooting from the bottom', did not suffer from nerves because

> I was only a kid and thought riding and going into the ring was just one of those things. But once I started to win a bit, my feelings gradually changed, especially when I turned professional and the money got so much bigger. It's become a much more serious business. I do get nerves now when I'm sitting waiting for a jump-off on a good horse and there's £2,000 or £3,000 to be won. It's very different from going for £100 at a small show.

The third day of the Olympia International Show Jumping Championships, in December 1978, was to prove an auspicious occasion for Nick who won three classes, culminating with the setting of a new British high-jump record. First, Maybe won the day's major jump-off class then Lastic took the Puissance. Afterwards a High Jump Record Challenge over poles was held:

> As the prize money was £2,000 I thought I'd have a go but I didn't start with enthusiasm or any great intention of breaking the record. Although Lastic would sometimes stop and shoot me off, he was basically a brave horse and once I had him running, he didn't turn his head to many jumps. I knew that if it suited him, he'd jump a double-decker bus if it was in his way.

The time before Nick's last try, when the poles were set at 7 feet $7\frac{5}{16}$ inches, Lastic demolished the lot. He picked up one stride too early, hit the jump half-way up and smashed it everywhere breaking two poles.

> Going down the last time, I was trying to go fairly quickly, but he was backing out on me although I was doing a lot of kicking. The last two strides I was kicking him as hard as I possibly could. He hit the boards at the bottom of the fence, then climbed and kept climbing and climbing till he'd got his front end over. I remember looking round at this moment and thinking, 'God,

Nick's penultimate attempt (LEFT) on the British high jump record resulted in a
matchstick situation . . .

. . . but Nick does not lack for courage. At his final attempt (RIGHT), at Olympia,
1978, Lastic went on to set a new record of 7 feet $7\frac{5}{16}$ inches. (*Both pictures
Findlay Davidson*)

the poles are still there.' Then I watched his back end come over.
He touched a pole which bounced and fell back into place. We
landed safely together and the record was ours.

To produce a world-beating performance, be the participant ath-
lete, tennis player or ballet dancer, all confess to being keyed-up
beforehand and Nick was no exception. After Lastic's disastrous
jump in the penultimate round Nick had felt desperately apprehensive about his final try:

I would have loved the lights to have gone out and the competition to have been abandoned. It's called fear. You'd be sure to

have nerves at that stage . . . I did anyway.

You never think in detail about what could happen at the time, but if you considered the possibilities of taking off wrong or hitting the fence half-way up it would be fateful. Someone above must have been on my side that night because miraculously both I and Lastic escaped all injury although we could have been killed. Of course crashing through didn't do Lastic's chances any harm. It both frightened and sharpened him up.

Between 1975, when Nick started jumping full-time, to the end of 1978, he progressed from a talented but raw newcomer, to regularly hitting the headlines in the senior league. Throughout these, his formative years, he had the invaluable asset of guidance from Ted and Liz.

Nick acknowledges,

Ted has one of the best eyes in the world for a show-jumper. He always tries to do a deal if the horse seems right, and seldom takes any of us with him. He likes to find jumpers and take the decision on his own. He's a great help to me on the floor. He tells me how to ride a particular horse, whether it should be faster, slower, nearer or further from a jump. There is no one better to tell me how to ride each horse. Liz has helped me most of all at the shows and with the courses. She excels at fences and strides.

There is no one like Ted with a difficult horse. He has a way with them. If I ask Ted for help, he gets on board, works the horse and when I get on afterwards, the horse goes perfectly. He does it totally by groundwork, just as much as is necessary.

Nick still rides If Ever the majority of the time because, after problems with an earlier rider, he is programmed to be difficult, but Ted can work him so that he is not nearly as headstrong and Nick can do what he wants with the enigmatical roan. Nick continues, 'After Ted has ridden Wallaby, he goes like a perfect gentleman for me, not in his normal wild-animal fashion.'

Nick usually travels to shows with Liz, as Ted makes only short visits to international shows. 'When I was a kid, Liz would always stick up for me and put things right when they went wrong.' As all parents with teenage children will appreciate, there were problems; times when Nick would fall out with Ted, especially in the winter, and Nick would go home and say he was leaving. 'I did this more than once and told my father I'd never go near Leek Wootton again. Sometimes I couldn't stand Ted.' David Skelton always took his recalcitrant son back, and Liz put matters right.

Nick remembers one such occasion:

> A week after I'd walked out, I eventually rang up Ted. Liz answered and said, 'He wants you to come for an interview at nine o'clock on Monday morning.' It was like going for another job, just as though I'd never been to Ponderosa before. I had to sit down and have a thorough talking to before I was allowed to start riding again.
>
> I think one reason I left so often was because I lived just down the road and it was all too easy. I only had to jump into the car and drive for a few minutes. It wouldn't have been so simple if home had been two hundred miles away.

There were also brighter days. When Nick first passed his driving test he often drove Ted. One day Ted asked Nick to take him to see his cousin in Warwick. They got into Nick's car, which was the apple of his eye, continually polished and kept like a Rolls-Royce. Nick recalls:

> When we had almost arrived, we had to turn round, so Ted jumped out saying he'd help me. Then, completely on purpose, he backed me straight into a lamp-post. I got out and 'coated' him. He laughed and said he hadn't done it on purpose, but I knew he had, and my car was left with a dented back wing.
>
> But I wasn't always right. Another time, Ted asked me to take him to a garage in Warwick to collect a lorry. I was driving down a steep hill through ice and snow towards a T-junction when Ted told me I was going too fast. 'Mind your own business,' I replied, 'I'm driving this car, not you.' No sooner had I said this than I attempted to put on my brakes, and I slid, and slid, and slid, over the junction, over the road, over the pavement and straight through a wall into someone's front garden. A man rushed out of the house and I jumped out of my car shouting, 'Why the hell don't you have a wire fence there like your neigh-

bour, not a brick wall?' The fellow shot back into his house. To
my surprise I'd frightened him to death.

The days of major rows ground to a halt during 1978 and, although
there are still occasionally the odd shouting matches, which is
healthy, the issues are minor and soon resolved.

At the onset of 1979, Nick's main campaigners were Jet Lag,
Maybe and Lastic, the latter being sold to Belgian François Mathy
in May of that year. Nick's season opened at Antwerp and then he
went on to Geneva where he was a member of the British team
and won the World Cup qualifier with Lastic. Nick had no previous
World Cup points, but this success, when a win carried only ten
points, as opposed to twenty in 1983, was sufficient to secure a
ticket to the first World Cup final in Gothenburg where he finished
seventh overall.

In its first five years, the World Cup has developed and become
an established Golden Grail and the first major competition bringing a purpose to the indoor season. Qualifying gives an edge to the
winter shows and Nick considers that the finals he has seen have
all been well run and with the right atmosphere.

Austria's Hugo Simon won the inaugural World Cup on Gladstone who was then at his peak. Gothenburg has become a show
to which Nick returns whenever possible, and not only because of
the good prize money. 'It's one of the best, because the people love
the show and go mad when we jump. It's just like being at a
football match.'

That August, Nick rode in his second Nations' Cup at Dublin
where Britain finished equal second with Germany to Ireland. All
season he was furthering his experience without sparking the highlights. Then, before Christmas, Nick was encouraged to find himself nominated as a member of the British team along with Lionel
Dunning, Mark Fuller and John Whitaker for the Zuidlaren International Horse Show in Holland. Britain won the Nations' Cup
which was contested by six countries.

For good measure, Maybe progressed to win the Grand Prix
and it was these two successes at the end of the season that marked
a rapidly maturing Nick as a likely candidate for the Moscow
Olympics in 1980. 1979 was a relatively quiet year as Nick gradually integrated into the senior scene.

It is not difficult to see why Maybe is Nick's favourite. (*Bob Langrish*)

Nick's 1980 highlight was to have been the Moscow Olympic Games and it remains one of his major disappointments that instead, he found himself riding with John Whitaker, Tim Grubb and Graham Fletcher in the Substitute Games in Rotterdam:

> We had to back Mrs Thatcher; there was no other way. But now I've turned professional and the Games look as far away as ever from becoming open, it seems most unlikely I'll ever get another shot at the individual gold medal. The Games should never have been given to Russia anyway.

FACING PAGE
Marie Edgar, at the age of eight, starting her winning ways on Franco.

It had been agreed behind the scenes that if the Games had been held in Moscow, Nick would ride David Broome's German grey Big Q, who, at that time, was certainly one of the most able

European horses. However, the plan never materialised because it was decided that Britain's riders would boycott the Moscow Games. So instead, Nick rode Maybe in the Substitute Games which inevitably lacked some of the aura of previous post-war equestrian Olympics.

Fourteen nations contested the Prix des Nations in Rotterdam where, as so often before, the again unheralded Canadians, led by veteran Jimmy Elder, popped up from behind to head Britain for the team gold medals.

Maybe achieved a double clear which was emulated by only two other horses: Damuraz (Mark Laskin) Canada, and Donau (Thomas Fruhmann) Austria. Nick remembers,

> It was unquestionably the biggest course I have ever seen in my life. I couldn't believe my eyes when I began to jump, especially when I approached the combination. No one had made it when my turn came, and the British and the German chef d'équipes had tried to stop me going into the ring because, after watching the previous riders, they had decided it was dangerous.

Horses such as Frederic Cottier's Flambeau, who has so much scope, had tipped up at the combination and even the giant Hanoverians favoured by the Germans were in difficulty, but Nick made little of the course and achieved the first clear. He explains,

> That combination was built for English horses. It was a parallel, with one long stride to a vertical in the middle, then two very short strides to a great big wide triple bar. That's what horses have to do in England all the time, shorten and open up.

So for Maybe and John Whitaker on Ryan's Son, who went on to take the silver individual medal, as well as a silver team medal, it was home from home, the type of question they had answered all their lives.

In autumn 1980, Nick went to s'Hertogenbosch in Holland and found himself in contention for the leading rider prize along with his friend Eddie Macken. The prizes were generous, cars to the first and second, a motor-bike for third and mopeds for fourth and fifth. Points from all the classes counted towards the cars and with

FACING PAGE
ABOVE LEFT Makedo at the gallop at the Wales and West, 1980. (*Bob Langrish*)

ABOVE RIGHT If Ever, winner of all three Grand Prix at Hickstead in 1982. (*Bob Langrish*)

BELOW Maybe and Radius enjoying their winter rest. (*Bob Langrish*)

one class to go, the Puissance, both Nick and Eddie were among those with a chance.

Nick had taken Barbarella for the big classes together with Jet Lag and Wallaby. Since Wallaby was inclined to stop and nap Nick restricted him mainly to speed clases. However, Nick recalls how Eddie persuaded him to enter Wallaby for the Puissance:

When Eddie first suggested the idea I replied, 'Don't be daft, I'll get killed. I'll have no chance.' Eddie, riding Freddy Welch's old horse Blossom Hill, continued, 'Come on, let's have a go and I'll bet you a fiver I'll jump higher than you do.' We battled on through two rounds and thirteen riders reached the third round including Eddie and me.

Unusually the wall was first, but it wasn't very big, only 6 feet 11 inches, but the parallel was huge and a more difficult fence than the wall. Eddie went first, had the wall down and hit the parallel. I was last to go and Eddie encouraged, 'Go on, you could make a name for yourself here and win a car.' Wallaby cleared the wall, as usual turned back very fast at the end of the ring with plenty of wheel spin, so I put on the brakes, then he shot back at full gallop to clear the parallel. He was the only one of the thirteen horses to jump the wall so he won the test and a Honda Civic car.

1981 was notable for the arrival of St James whom Ted bought from his brother-in-law, David Broome, for Terry Clemence. An Irish-bred gelding who started his jumping career in the West Country as Sunny Side Up, he was bought by David who then changed his name to Harris Home Care. Perhaps the name, redolent of a sink scourer, had denigrated him in his rider's mind. However, the liver chestnut won countless classes for David, but usually as second string.

Happily, the horse's name was changed to St James as Terry Clemence is a member of the consortium who originally backed this very successful upper-echelon London residential club.

St James was delivered to Ted during the World Cup final at Birmingham, in 1982. He won his first competition with Nick in the saddle, a £50 Open Class at Knebworth Park in Hertfordshire, the following week.

At that time, Nick thought St James was a good horse. Then, as now, he was very careful and tried his best, but Nick never dreamed he would clear the fences he now does. Conversely, Ted had always thought that St James possessed plenty of unrealised and unexploited ability. This reveals why there was a broad grin on Ted's face on a cold, wet, muddy May Bank Holiday afternoon when Nick and St James finished second to David on Tabac Original at the Colt Car Spring Fair at Amberley near Cirencester. The course had been big and St James had responded to a younger more thrusting rider, just as Ted had anticipated, with a display of hitherto unexposed scope.

St James' wins then followed thick and fast. In just eight weeks, he carried Nick to the championships at Royal Windsor and the Surrey and Suffolk County Shows, the South of England, the first leg of the Amateur Championship at Cardiff, and then the National Championship at the Royal.

> I soon discovered that he had a great mind to clear the fences, and touch wood, to this day, he has never failed to make any big fence. Somehow he finds a way of getting over without touching anything. When I feel a combination is huge, St James treats it as a mole-hill.

After this brilliant run, a bitter pill was to follow at the Royal International where Nick had set his heart on winning the King George V Gold Cup: 'It was the biggest disappointment of my life because St James was going so well I thought I had a real chance.'

After turning a corner, St James lowered the pole from a big parallel. His legs barely grazed the jump, Nick did not hear the pole fall and had cleared the next fence before he realised the pole had gone. St James made no further error and was very easily fast enough to have won. David Broome, who can never ever be ignored, came through to achieve his fifth King's Cup victory with Mr Ross, Derek Ricketts was second on Hydrophane Coldstream and St James was third.

Two nights later, St James atoned to a degree by winning the John Player Grand Prix, and then the Everest Supreme Championship on the final day. Although St James and Nick were the show's leading horse and rider with £9,945 to their credit, followed by Liz and Forever with £4,741, the memory of the King's Cup still rankled: 'I could have spat fire that night.'

Form at the Royal International is usually influential in the selection of the team for Dublin. Two weeks later, St James was a member of the British team who finished a disappointing third in the Nations' Cup behind Germany and Switzerland.

St James's next international was at Calgary in Alberta where Nick won a Power and Speed Class on Carat, but this proved scant consolation for failing in the Grand Prix. The first untimed jump-off fence was a vertical with masses of trees, bushes and flowers in front. Looking back, Nick says, 'I thought it was impossible to hit it, but I was wrong again and gave the class away. Although it measured only 4 feet 6 inches high, down it came so I had four faults. David went on to win with Philco and collected £7,000.'

For Nick, the 1982 Horse of the Year Show was momentous for two reasons. He won the Servis Spurs for the leading rider on points. Then, after winning the *Horse and Hound* Cup on the final night with Carat, Nick announced his engagement to Shropshire international Sarah Edwards. With £4,585 to their credit, he and St James were third to Malcolm Pyrah (Towerlands Anglezarke) and David Broome (Mr Ross) in the show's leading money-winners' list.

St James' arrival in the Edgars' stables in 1981 could not have been more timely because Maybe suffered a leg injury at Aachen that June. It showed up the day after a competition, and while Nick didn't feel it happen, he thinks it may have occurred at the permanent bank which is surmounted by a privet hedge. On that occasion there was also a pole over the hedge and Maybe cleared it by two feet, making such an enormous effort that he jumped some seven feet high. He then landed very steeply and probably incurred the leg injury in doing so. He was fired in front and subsequently out of action, resting and recuperating, for the remainder of 1981.

He next came out in 1982 at Newark in May and everything seemed all right until the Royal in July when he slipped over behind as Nick turned him, injuring a tendon in his back leg. That had to be fired which side-lined him until the Heythrop Show the following spring which show-jumper Richard Sumner runs on his farm near Chipping Norton.

Nick dreaming of what might have been, seen here with his friend John Whitaker (left) in a Shetland pony race at Olympia. (*Kit Houghton*)

The Swedish chestnut, Everest Carat, proved an excellent back-up horse in 1981 winning many speed classes. He had had several different riders in his time and was finally jumped by Ireland's Paul Darragh before he came to England. By then, he had developed an all-too-frequent stop which has been almost eradicated.

On 15th February, 1982, Nick took a major step and turned professional. He made this decision because he was hoping to get married before the end of the year and now that he was very much on level terms with his more senior rivals, Everest were understandably anxious to derive maximum publicity from his wins. If he relinquished his amateur status, their horses could carry the Everest prefix in competition.

The season opened with a blow for Nick when he learnt that St James, who had gone back to his owner's Essex home for his winter rest, was not to be returned to be prepared for the season.

This was because Mr Clemence's daughter, Sarah-Jane, who was eligible for young riders' classes, decided she would like to jump him herself.

But although St James has every intention of clearing fences if he meets them on the right stride, he is by no means an easy ride: he runs very strongly, pulls and is always changing legs behind. He is a brilliant but difficult horse for any young rider – even a winning one like Sarah-Jane – who wants to make the transition to senior classes.

St James began putting in the odd stop, including one with Nick when he was offered the ride at the 1982 July Hickstead meeting. Sarah-Jane had him back again and he continued to put in the occasional refusal. Then Mr Clemence asked Ted if he would take on the horse while the family went on holiday. During that time Nick took him to Dinard where he won a class, then to Millstreet in County Cork where he won the Irish Derby over a course which Hickstead course designer, Pamela Carruthers, who was judging, rated bigger than the Hickstead equivalent.

But St James' yo-yo base pattern continued and Mr Clemence then had him home again. He refused again with Sarah-Jane so he was returned to Ted in time for the Everest Championships at Park Farm, Northwood, where he proceeded to put in a really dirty stop with Nick on the first day. Thereafter Nick proceeded to square him up in time for the Horse of the Year Show the following week, where polished and cool, he won the Leading Show Jumper of the Year title.

Nick had sorted out his differences with St James with a vengeance and he reigned supreme in the crowded arena as Dorian Williams read Ronald Duncan's emotive tribute *The Horse*, with £17,600 to his credit – £7,600 prize money won by St James with the £10,000 Peugeot car awarded the show's leading rider, ready to drive away. The year of ups and downs ended on a happy note with St James winning both the Grand Prix and World Cup Qualifier at the Indoor Dublin Show and the Olympia Grand Prix.

Not having St James for the bulk of the season meant that Nick had to rely much more on If Ever. The first time he saw If Ever was at Vienna, in 1980, in a speed class which Nick was winning with Jet Lag by a second. Nick couldn't believe his eyes because If Ever (then called Epsom) was running away, right out of control, missing out strides everywhere. He thought no more about it until at Gothenburg, both Liz and Nick saw the horse in the puissance where the parallel in the last round reached enormous dimensions. Nick recalls, 'Epsom turned the corner and stood back one stride too early. I just looked away, certain he would crash it but incredibly he made the seven-feet spread.'

When he arrived home, Nick told Ted of the horse he'd seen ridden by a Belgian boy who, although not very big (15.3 h.h.), and really difficult, was brilliant. Soon afterwards, François Mathy told Ted on the phone that he had Epsom in his stables and Ted asked Nick if he knew the horse. 'Yes,' replied Nick, 'it's the roan I told you about. I should go to Belgium and buy it.' Ted went and after seeing the horse jump, bought him. He is French-bred – a Selle Français – by Nankin out of Quassia who is by Furioso. In colour he is a rare red roan.

Nick looked forward to Epsom's arrival but ...

When he came home, the fun began; he needed some taming! I battled along with him for a bit but had no success at all. Ted said we'd have to make or break him, so one day we set about him and worked and worked him on the flat. Soon afterwards, I took him to the Wales and West Show and he jumped two clear rounds.

If Ever, as he was renamed although his stable name remains Epsom, possesses a huge natural jump and is careful, but he was certainly not an indoor or Wembley horse at that stage because his stride could not be altered sufficiently quickly and he was still very awkward.

In 1981, If Ever was taken gently, achieving some minor placings here and there. Ted and Nick felt sure that one day he would make a good horse, so they did not give up when others would have done so. In 1982 their persistence and patience was rewarded. Nevertheless, to this day he remains difficult and although he was still improving in 1983, Nick can never guarantee what he will do. During the World Championships at Dublin in June 1982, which were an absolute disaster for the British team, Nick wished he could have turned ostrich and buried his head in the sand. He says: 'If Ever could quite easily have jumped a clear every day, but

instead he was eliminated in the first round after a desperate struggle at a double off a corner, then only had the last down in the second round.'

But only two weeks later at the end of June in Aachen, If Ever most adequately atoned for his Dublin disgrace when he and Nick followed in the shoes of Liz on Forever and Malcolm Pyrah with Towerlands Anglezarke and became the third consecutive British combination to win the prestigious Grosser Preis von Aachen.

Happily, the good days easily outnumbered the bad in 1982, as If Ever established a remarkable record, winning the three Hickstead Grand Prix. He shared the first in May with David Broome on Mr Ross, with the European Championship combination of Paul Schockemohle and Deister third, and was the sole winner of the June and July contests, collecting a total of £19,750 for these three efforts.

Riders from eleven nations contested the Everest Double Glazing Grand Prix on Spring Bank Holiday Monday when Nick came home through a six-horse jump-off by 0.1 second to deny World Cup holder Melanie Smith and Calypso from the United States the £7,000 first prize and delight sponsor David Kingsley.

Some of Nick's greatest assets are that he can take criticism and maintain a good working relationship with Ted and Liz, remembering to say thank you when things go well. More often than not he goes better when Ted or Liz are at a show with him, probably because their presence and advice boosts his confidence. If Nick is away on his own he frequently phones back two or three times a day, both to report progress and to seek direction.

Well over the poles, Nick is already plotting his route to the next fence at the Royal Agricultural Show on St James in 1983. (*Kit Houghton*)

CHAPTER FOUR

LESLEY McNAUGHT

Lesley's family had always had some ponies and horses about so they feature in her earliest memories of home. Her grandmother usually kept at least two horses for her mother and aunt, so Lesley automatically found herself on the back of an old Welsh 12.2 h.h. bay pony called Curiosity that her mother had ridden before her.

Mrs McNaught was Lesley's first teacher and her pupil was soon competing on the bay gelding in leading-rein classes. Lesley's home was at Burbage, a little village near Hinckley in Leicestershire, where her mother had a small farm and rented out forty acres to a local farmer to grow wheat.

She was brought up by her mother because her father left home when she was only four or five years old and she can only vaguely remember him. Lesley is not a Catholic, but went to St Albert's Convent, a private junior school in Hinckley, progressing to the John Cleveland College in the same town.

Lesley has one sister, Helen, who is three years younger than she is. In 1983, Helen spent some time working with horses in Ireland with a dealer called Con McIlroy and enjoyed the experience away from home, partly because it is not easy to follow such an illustrious sister. Although she is across the Irish sea, Helen remains quite close to Lesley and they keep in touch by fairly regular talks on the telephone.

In 1977, before Liz first saw Lesley in action, Lesley had a very good 13.2 h.h. pony called Golden Arrow who was quite old, either twelve or thirteen, when Mrs McNaught first bought him. He missed qualifying for Wembley by only one place, finishing equal fourth with Robert Smith on Shropshire Lad in his Regional Final. Lesley rates him a 'fantastic pony; he won some very good classes. I was especially fond of him because he always tried his heart out for me.' The pony is still going strong now, carrying and teaching another little girl down Hereford way. Sister Helen rode Golden Arrow after Lesley.

Lesley always wanted to ride as a career but never thought it would be possible. Then Liz approached her mother after having seen Lesley ride at Hilton Park in 1977. That day, Dave Dick told Liz, 'If you want to see a good kid ride, watch this one.' Lesley McNaught happened to be going in to compete in a 13.2 h.h. class on a 12 h.h. pony that had just been eliminated with Helen in the saddle. Lesley was thirteen years old and from the way she rode the pony, Liz knew instantly that Lesley 'had the gift'. The pony had stopped only a few minutes earlier and now it was jumping fluent clear rounds.

Liz asked Mrs McNaught to see if her daughter might like to ride for them when eventually she left school. Then Lesley was introduced to Ted and she immediately showed interest in joining them. The following winter, Ted and Liz had a young horse called Wurzel that they wanted to give experience in restricted classes, for which they, as international riders, were not eligible. They suggested that Lesley could jump him and she readily accepted.

The first class in which Lesley rode Wurzel was a Midland Bank qualifier at Stoneleigh when she had three clears, finished third and qualified for the final. The following Tuesday, she rode Wurzel at Balsall Common in a Winter Riders' Class, finishing equal first. She then went with him to the Basildon Bond final the following Saturday finishing second, 'after making a complete and utter mess of the competition'.

Lesley recalls that early show:

The rider in the lead wasn't all that fast, but I went along as though I had all the time in the world, missed the turn to the second fence wasting about three seconds, when I heard Ted shouting, 'Get a move on!' At last, I did, but it was too late and I was beaten by one-tenth of a second. I'd have won if only I'd moved on from the start. Instead I received my first bawl out from Ted, for dawdling!

That summer Ted gave Lesley the ride on a pony called Skipalong. The pony went really well and won a Christy Beaufort Qualifier

Lesley will surely treasure her memories of One More Time. (*Bob Langrish*)

before she was sold. During the winter of 1978-79, Liz's sister, Mary Broome, was looking for a good jockey to ride Shipley Hills, the pony she owned jointly with her mother, and asked her sister if she knew of one. Liz did not hesitate – she arranged for Lesley and her mother to meet Mary and a deal was struck. Throughout 1979 Lesley jumped Shipley Hills who was kept at Burbage.

Golden Arrow and Skipalong were well above-average ponies but Shipley Hills was Lesley's first top-ranking mount:

> He was a class pony but had continually refused for two years after being sold by Paul Miles. In all honesty, I never went against the clock with him until after June the year that we had him, I just rode him tactfully and had no problem, aiming him for clear rounds which I usually achieved because he was very careful.

Shipley Hills' best win was probably the Bicton Derby, which is held near Exeter. Lesley also won the Victor Ludorum. At the Horse of the Year Show, she finished fourth in the Leading Junior

Jumper of the Year Competition to Caroline Thomas on Reveille
and registered an extremely fast time.

To head the BSJA leading pony money-winner of the year list is
no mean feat in this hotly contested category. Lesley justified her
decision to make horses her career when Shipley Hills won this
title in 1979.

Shipley Hills was then sold, passing through the hands of Jet
Taylor and Mr Heffer before being jumped by Anthony Hopkin-
son in the north of England. Sadly, in 1982, he succumbed to an
attack of colic and died in his stable.

Looking back in March 1983, Lesley said,

> I have learnt so much from Ted and Liz, but one point that
> stands out is Ted's advice on shows: 'Do your own thing and
> don't listen to collecting ring prattle,' as he puts it. 'There's no
> point being influenced by what the other riders plan to do
> because everyone has not only a different horse, but also a
> different approach.' Ted is very good at helping with a jump in
> the collecting ring just before I go into the ring to sharpen up a
> horse and make sure it is going right. Liz is really outstanding
> on distances and explaining exactly how a fence should be
> ridden.

Lesley explains that Ted and Liz have both helped her enormously
with the groundwork which is vital to successful show-jumping,
but in slightly different ways: 'Liz used to spend much time teaching me how to get something right, and whereas Ted would tell me
too, he was usually more inclined to get on the horse I was trying
to school and show me how to do it that way.'

At the same time, Liz has much to say of Lesley's qualities as a
rider: 'She's a total natural, with an exceptional eye and is prodi-
giously strong.' 'Strong as an ox,' reinforces Ted, 'so she can hold
any horse together. She is also as cool as a cucumber.'

The essential element of luck also played its part in Lesley's life,
because if Liz had not seen the young hopeful compete at Hilton
Park, she would probably never have had the opportunity to ride
with Ted and Liz. Lesley is quick to learn and realising the chance
that had come her way, seized it, turning it to full advantage and
letting nothing slip.

During the winter of 1979–80, Lesley attended school as little as possible, usually turning up at Elms Farm on Friday afternoon or night, hoping for rides over the weekend, and going home on Sunday night or Monday morning in time for school. This continued until Lesley's sixteenth birthday on 10th February, when she abruptly left school before the end of term and came to ride full-time for Ted and Liz, living as one of the family.

That first year, she rode the little mare Whenever, a horse called Whyever and had a few rides on the then novice Radius, as well as another novice, Mexico.

To start with, Ted usually travelled with her as Nick was away at World Cup Qualifiers most of the time. Those first months she competed largely indoors at Stoneleigh, Hereford and Balsall Common.

Lesley remembers how she felt at the time,

> My mother was really pleased that I was going to be able to follow my chosen career; I knew what a good stable I was coming to and hoped to do my best. Even when I was thirteen years old, I was quite aware that Ted and Liz Edgars' horses were outstanding.

On the 1980 outdoor circuit Lesley, more often than not accompanied by Ted, began widening her experience at county-type shows, competing at such venues as Stafford County and the City of Manchester. The Royal International was not on the list, but she was second in the Whitbread Young Riders' Championship. She rode Whato for Liz at the Chippenham and Charlton Show in April when he won the Grade B and Grade C Classes, and she more or less kept him from then onwards. But it was Liz who had given Whato his initial training and brought him up to Grade B. Whato has always been a fizzy horse who tends to hot up in competitions, but on the plus side he has one of the biggest jumps in the sport, so his limitation is mental rather than physical. In the stable anyone can do anything with him.

Lesley also had a few placings with Hardly Ever at the 1980 Horse of the Year Show. She had qualified him at Monmouth earlier in the season by winning the Welsh Championship. This

Lesley and One More Time winning the British Ladies Championship at the 1981 Royal Windsor Horse Show. (*Findlay Davidson*)

was a year when Lesley was 'learning all the time, just as I still am; you are always learning in jumping. In 1980, I learnt most about strides and schooling on the flat.'

Half-way through the year, Ted had bought a little mare called One More Time because he thought she was just the type to win Lesley the European Junior Championship the following year. He chose One More Time because although she is not the scopiest horse, she jumps sufficiently big, is super careful, and, above all, fast; speed is nearly always crucial in this Junior Championship. It was in July that Lesley first competed on One More Time and she won the North of England Grade B Championship at Manchester. Then, only a fortnight later, she won the Grade B Championship at Harlow which upgraded One More Time to Grade A.

That autumn, Lesley went to her first show abroad, Le Vaudreuil, in France, where she made her foreign debut with a degree of panache by winning the Grand Prix with One More Time. Without Ted or Liz there to advise her, for the first time at a competition of this level Lesley had to make her own decisions about jumping. To this day, one of her favourite sweaters is a navy one with 'Le Vaudreuil' emblazoned across the front.

Meanwhile, like Lesley, Whato had been progressing up the ladder: in 1980 he won the Open Championship at Harlow and the Adult Championship at the Southport Flower Show. Lesley was gaining confidence as she discovered she could hold her own not only against her contemporaries, but also in lesser classes on the national circuit.

From the start, her activities included grooming and feeding her horses, doing the tack and keeping the front of the lorry clean. Nick is usually responsible for the horses' area. Lesley also really loved being in the house with Liz, helping her get dinner ready and keeping the kitchen tidy. The kitchen is the hub of Rio Grande and always busy.

It will be a long time before another seventeen-year-old collects a triumvirate of major victories as Lesley did in 1981. The first was the Ladies National title at the Royal Windsor Horse Show in May. Lesley had expected to be riding Whato, but just before declarations closed, Ted correctly decided that in relation to the entries, the likely course and the going would favour One More Time and entered her instead.

In June on the last day of the Three Counties Show at Malvern, One More Time won the Power and Speed Class in the morning, and in the afternoon the Show Championship. Ted thought it would be good if she could have a chance to ride in the Amateur Championship at Cardiff as she was going so well. Liz phoned the show secretary and found that as they were short of entries Lesley would be accepted.

After a desperate scurry home to Leek Wootton to get some clothes for three days and wash breeches overnight, Liz drove Lesley to Cardiff and she won the Amateur Championship with One More Time.

Then in August, came the adventure and excitement of winning the Junior European Championship in Switzerland, also with One More Time. In spring 1983, at the time of writing, Lesley considered it one of the two most thrilling days of her life.

At the Everest Double Glazing Show at Park Farm, Northwood, that September (1981) Lesley had the ride on FMS Barbarella because Nick could not ride her at the Horse of the Year Show at Wembley the following week. This was because he had qualified five horses and the limit is three horses for one rider. This meant that Lesley would have the ride at Wembley instead of Nick. After finishing equal first in a class at the Everest Show with Michael Whitaker and Disney Way, she was equal second with Michael's eldest brother John on Ryan's Son in the Leading Show Jumper of the Year competition at Wembley, which was won by David Broome on Mr Ross.

1982 opened and ended on a high note. Lesley won the Lancia car in the final Lancia Championship at Park Farm, with FMS Barbarella. Although she could drive, she did not pass her test until 25th November that year, so she sat in the passenger seat and let a Lancia chauffeur take her on her victory circuit. As Lesley was an amateur, the car, as all her winnings, went to Ted for the horse's owner, Cliff Cox. After Lesley passed her test, Ted and Liz let her borrow a car any time she needed one.

At the Royal Windsor Horse Show in the Ladies' National Championship, Lesley was clear initially on One More Time, but missed a fence and had to stop. This she put down to trying too hard in the jump-off instead of heeding Liz's advice: 'Never go beyond your own capabilities, only aim to achieve what you know you can do.' Liz went on to win with Forever.

In the Queen Elizabeth II Cup at the Royal International Horse Show in July, the jump-off was between Liz and Forever and Lesley who opened on Barbarella. Lesley says that Barbarella is a mare who doesn't like a lot of affection but is always very genuine and controllable. She recalls what happened:

Once again I learnt by my mistakes. If I'd had any sense, I'd have aimed for a clear, instead I went daft, tried to cut a dash and had two fences down, leaving the Cup wide open for Liz who had a steady clear and won with Forever. I shan't do that again in a hurry. Just occasionally such riding comes off and you are a hero. More often it doesn't and you feel an idiot.

At the Horse of The Year Show in 1982, Lesley is concentrating hard on Barbarella as she receives last-minute orders from Ted on the way to the ring. (*Kit
Houghton*)

Lesley did get some compensation by winning the *Daily Mail* Cup
on FMS Barbarella against some tough competition. But she has
never been over-awed by riding against famous more-experienced
competitors: 'I just go in and try to do my best, riding against the
course and the clock and never counting my chickens before they
are hatched.' Malcolm Pyrah was second on Towerlands Anglezarke, and third, Paul Schockemohle on Akrobat.

But, if failing to win the Queen Elizabeth II Cup was not a
crushing blow, failing to retain the Junior European Championship was, and One More Time showed some useful form at the
Royal International winning the Lancôme Speed Class.

As defending European Junior Champion, Lesley's place at the
Championship was assured. All season she had been looking forward to the event which was to be held at Le Vaudreuil in France.
After having won the Grand Prix there two years earlier, she felt
this was a fortuitous omen. Showjumper Anne Newbery travelled

with her but, as Lesley says, 'in 1982, One More Time never quite hit the same form she showed throughout 1981. She won the opening class, then the next day she would have won if she hadn't lowered the last fence, and she was by no means galloping full tilt.'

In the Nations' Cup, One More Time produced the requisite two clear rounds, which were to no avail as two of Lesley's fellow team members fell off. France won and Britain were right out of the hunt.

Lesley never gave up hope of keeping the individual title. One More Time jumped a cracking first round and was again faultless in the second round although she did not jump as well:

> Looking back, I just wish there had not been a third round or we might have made it with only two.
>
> Pulling her out a third time, she had a parallel down going into the double so I slowed her down a bit and she finished in fifth place, three seconds behind Jonathan Egmore who won the gold individual medal for Britain on Postmark. I was really disappointed with my result and tried to comfort myself with the thought that many of the riders I admired had never had the luck to win the title once ... but it didn't help me very much at the time.

With her final opportunity to ride in the European Junior Championships behind her, Lesley's first CSI as a full senior was at the Horse of the Year Show in October 1982 and she did not let the occasion go by unrecorded.

She was not unduly disturbed by competing as a full-time senior and in her first ever Puissance she rode Whato and tied for first place with Harvey Smith on Sanyo Technology.

Thereafter, Lesley and Whato proceeded to establish themselves as Puissance specialists winning the following week at the Autumn Championships at Stoneleigh where she jumped higher than at Wembley, clearing 7 feet 2 inches. Then she was equal first at Dublin with Lt John Ledingham on Sliabh-na-mBan, equal first on Whato in the Cognac Courvoisier Bareback High Jump Challenge at Olympia with Austrian Thomas Fruhmann on Bandit, then equal second with three others, on Whato, in the Radio Rentals Puissance behind Switzerland's Thomas Fuchs on Willora

Swiss. In 1983 at Antwerp, she and Whato were equal first with Walter Gabathuler on Beethoven. This meant that in their first six Puissances, Lesley and Whato had achieved the fine record of five firsts and a second.

Seven feet two inches is the maximum Lesley cleared on Whato but she always felt that if she could calm him sufficiently, he could go higher. 'I wish the jump could go higher earlier, because in the first rounds he gets increasingly buzzy.'

'Winning my first Grand Prix was a big occasion,' but riding down to a massive wall on Whato presented, 'touch wood, no worries because I always felt he would take off and clear the jump when I asked him, which was a great confidence booster and helped the pair of us over.'

Life at the Royal International and Horse of the Year Shows was made easier for Lesley in 1982 as she had someone to do her horses. Also she went up to the Crest Hotel for dinner with Ted and Liz each night after jumping, before returning to sleep in the horsebox.

Lesley was very sorry to lose the ride on One More Time at the end of 1982 because she is her favourite horse to date and because she had had the mare from Grade B:

> When you've brought a horse through to Grade A and it has gone on to become a regular winner, it gives so much more satisfaction than stepping onto a ready-made horse. One More Time is also really genuine, consistent and always tried her best for me. She is brave and fast, even without going against the clock, so I always knew I was in with a first-class chance of winning, if I could reach the jump-off.

As a novice the mare was ridden by Anna Fawdry and owned by Michael Lysart. Irish-bred, she is by Stone Fox. When Lesley was out of Young Riders' Classes, to which the mare was best suited, One More Time was sold to another young rider called Julie Salt who lives in Coventry. Julie comes over to ride One More Time each evening after school as she is still kept at Rio Grande.

In February 1983 Ted sent Lesley on holiday with Liz and Liz's sister Mary to Thailand for a fortnight because he thought the change would do her good.

Wally appears to be taking a short rest on the top of the wall at Birmingham, 1983, but he went on to win this Puissance. (*Kit Houghton*)

In common with most of her generation, in the evening Lesley enjoys a good meal out and then going on to a disco. Inevitably, because show-jumping is a full and demanding life, most of her friends are at least peripherally connected with horses, and she considers Zoe Bates one of those closest to her. She loves shopping for clothes, and most of all enjoys collecting smart casual outfits.

CHAPTER FIVE

HIGHLIGHTS OF CAREERS

TED

Like all riders, Ted carries memories of certain competitions that have meant more to him than any others:

> Ever since I was a kid I wanted to win the Grand National, the Derby or the King's Cup. The Derby proved impossible because I was so heavy. I never did get the chance to ride ESB who went on to Grand National victory, so my big aim was to come back after being suspended and win the King's Cup. Even now, in 1983, when the competition has gone back out of doors again to the White City, I reckon it's the greatest individual class to win.
>
> It's hard to explain why it means so much – the prize-money is hardly sensational – but even the foreigners want to win that class. All those of my generation, like Dougie Bunn who was second several times, wanted to win. I set my heart on success because I knew that if you were anyone you won the King's.

The night preceding the King George V Gold Cup competition, back in 1969, Ted was second in the *Horse and Hound* Cup; he went to bed early in preparation to achieve his life's ambition.

The competition took place outside under the stars at Wembley football stadium: 'When I walked the course, I knew I could not win because there was a double of parallels with nine yards inside and Uncle Max could not get distance.' It was the worst fence that could ever have been included for Uncle Max and Ted thought it most unlikely he could fit in two strides.

Ted and Max bravely attacked the course and reached the jump-off against the clock. The fences, including the double, went up again and Ted was drawn first. His only chance of survival was to sacrifice a few seconds and follow the same track to the double as before. His timing was perfect: in, one long stride and out, and over the wall to finish. A clear round but six top horses to follow.

Ted takes up the story:

It was agony watching them all try to beat me, especially as Harvey, who went last, had me on the clock; he shot through the combination, but got wrong at the wall.

As I realised I'd won I threw my hat and coat in the air. I'll never forget walking up those steps where the football cup finalists go, to meet the Queen, and the Duke of Beaufort whom I had already met. I sensed that Dougie Bunn was a little envious because he so badly wanted to win. 'You want to tidy up and comb your hair if you are going up there,' he said. 'Piss off,' I replied, 'the Duke's up there and he'll speak to me anyway.' When I arrived up there he said, 'I know this is the one you really wanted to win.' I felt ten feet tall as I replied, 'You are right, your Grace.'

Especially satisfying in Ted's mind was the impressive list of runners-up. Alwin Schockemohle, later to win the Olympic individual gold medal with Warwick, was equal second on the almost unbeatable Donald Rex, tying with Lutz Merkel on Anmut. Harvey Smith was seventh with Mattie Brown.

Afterwards Ted was interviewed by his friend, television commentator David Coleman, who asked him how he managed to get on so well with Uncle Max when so many others had failed. Ted, the incorrigible, replied, 'Because we are two right bastards together.' Coleman hiccupped but before he could drop his microphone the remark had gone out live across the nation.

Not surprisingly, Ted went out on a blinder of a celebration party in the stadium led by Irish show-jumpers Tommy Brennan and Leslie Fitzpatrick. Dawn was breaking as Ted was pushed back down the hill in a handcart to his caravan, by a group of revellers. Ted Williams, a member of the party, had somehow been locked in the stadium, on the fourth floor. Cries of 'Help! Are you going to leave me here all night?' eventually resulted in his extrication.

His proudest moment. Ted receiving the coveted St George and the Dragon
Trophy from the Queen, after winning the King George V Gold Cup at the 1969
Royal International Horse Show. Prince Philip, Princess Margaret, Lord Snow-
don and the Duke of Beaufort are among the onlookers. (*Monty*)

Ted, during and after his daring and intrepid ride on Jacapo, following which he received a special champagne award from the Master of Hickstead, Douglas Bunn, for completing a one-armed attack on the Derby Course in 1963. (left, *Jean Bridel*)

One feat of already legendary valour that cannot go unrecorded was Ted's ride on Jacapo in the 1963 Hickstead Derby. Three weeks before the competition he began preparing Jacapo, and was especially keen to succeed because all his friends and rivals said he could not do so with this horse.

Three days beforehand Ted's plans went totally awry when a young horse he was breaking in shot him out of the saddle kicking his elbow out of its socket in the process.

On his way to Hickstead he stopped off in London and had the bones put back into place, but the swelling was so extensive he couldn't even get his shirt on. The only possible way for Ted to compete over the formidable sixteen-fence Derby course, which included a steep 10 feet 6 inches drop off a bank, was one-handed with the other arm in a sling.

Then, as now, the Master of Hickstead is not slow to recognise courage, or a stunning chance of publicity, so he duly offered Ted a crate of champagne if he could get round. Ted, imbued with the heart of a lion and never one to resist such a challenge, achieved the impossible and finished in the placings with only eight faults to the wild acclaim of the crowd.

LIZ

The Aachen Grand Prix, the Grosser Preis von Aachen, is one of the world's most prestigious classes and at the start of the 1983 season it rated as Liz's most important win on Forever.

Liz found herself in Aachen in June 1980 as a member of a team of amateurs who were sent there as part of their preparation for the Substitute Olympics in Rotterdam.

The one exception was professional Malcolm Pyrah who was detailed by chef d'équipe Ronnie Massarella to advise on how to cope in Aachen. As this was Liz's initial visit, the minute she arrived on the showground she sought his help. She was very apprehensive about this trip but was reassured to a degree because her brother David felt that Forever would 'find himself in Aachen'.

Years beforehand, Liz had been to Aachen with Ted and seen how big the courses were – Forever had not:

> The first course Forever jumped in Aachen, he couldn't believe the width of the parallels and almost put his back feet down a couple of them. Malcolm kept saying don't worry about it, he'll soon realise they are that bit bigger and cope. How right he was.

By the Nations' Cup he had completely adjusted, registering a two-round total of four faults, the equal British best with Robert Smith and Video. Thirteen Nations' Cup teams competed; France won and Britain were fifth.

After a rest on Saturday, Liz just qualified for the Grosser Preis von Aachen. She was drawn very early on to face a gruelling first round over thirteen fences, including an enormous double at the far end of the ring with an entry parallel that was, 'one to remem-

ber. If you cleared that parallel, you had a chance of going clear.'
Liz need not have worried. Forever met this fence, where many
hopes were dashed, absolutely right.

Three fences were removed for the second round but the double
was not one of them. Five horses remained for the fourth round,
the second and final jump-off against the clock. Liz was drawn first
to go over a course of six single fences dotted all over the ring.

Ted arrived just in time for the Grand Prix, and Liz, who had
already walked the course, greeted him with a masterly understate-
ment: 'If you want to see something, go and look at the course –
it's big.'

Liz takes up the story:

> As I went into the ring Ted advised me not to go too daft and
> just to do my best. I'd looked at the other four riders and
> thought I'd finish fifth. I don't know what possessed me but I
> set off at a gallop. It was the first time anyone had ever seen
> Forever really gallop and I went absolutely flat out. He jumped
> like a 'chaser and came home clear in 46.6 seconds.

John Whitaker took second place for Britain, by finishing clear on
Ryan's Son in 50.3 seconds; and third, with the only other faultless
round in 51.6 seconds, was Spain's Alfonso Segovia on Agamem-
non.

Forever had extended his stride so smoothly that the speed at
which he travelled was not easily perceptible but when two fast
combinations – Livius (Peter Luther) for West Germany, and
Harley (Walter Gabathuler) for Switzerland, third and second the
previous year – collected eight and four faults respectively in slower
times, the penny dropped.

The 45,000 capacity crowd that had crammed into the Reitur-
nierplatz, hoping to see national hero Paul Schockemohle and El
Paso, who had won the previous year, complete a Grand Prix
double, rose to their feet wildly applauding Liz, the first ever lady
victor, and Forever who, as a face-saver, was at least German-
bred.

At the time, Liz did not quite appreciate the importance of her
victory. It was a hot afternoon and she had found it a sickening
experience to have to ask Forever to go a fourth time:

Usually the horse will have finished after a second round; a third he will put up with; but a fourth time is asking too much and taking advantage of his good nature.

Ted told me to go and give him a jump but I wasn't sure he needed one. 'Go and give him one jump,' Ted insisted, 'so he knows he's going in the arena to jump and not for a presentation.'

I walked him the length of paddock, had one jump, thought about pulling out but decided I wouldn't, having got through three rounds, stoked him up and went in determined to have a real try. Of course I was very pleased but I was also rather disgusted that I'd used Forever to that extent. Still, he came up with all the answers.

Although the Aachen win was the most prestigious, the victory that has given Liz most satisfaction in a plenitude of wins is Forever's Sanyo Talent Spotters' Championship at the National Equestrian Centre Autumn Championships in 1978. Anyone who has a nice young horse always wants to prove their point and this competition provided the ideal opportunity.

First there was the drama of qualifying because in the initial year of the competition, there were only four qualifying rounds. Forever qualified at the Wales and West Show in July by finishing third. The first four went through to the final.

With the first trauma over, the final soon loomed up at Stoneleigh in October. It was a two-round competition. Course builder Alan Ball had set quite a respectable course for the first round, but for the second it was very big for horses of this level of experience, and included a wall at 5 feet 6 inches with small white bricks on the top.

Four horses provided the double clears necessary to reach the jump-off when the fences were minimally lowered to allow the horses to have a go. South African Peter Gotz (formerly married to 1976 Olympic rider Debbie Johnsey) opened with twelve faults on Invitation. David Broome followed on Sunnyside Up, with a clear in 35.1 seconds. Liz then captured the class with a fluent round in which Forever was not unduly extended as he passed the finish without fault two seconds faster than Sunnyside Up. The talented Scot, John Brown, was third on Fymac.

'It was a super class to win because I'd fulfilled all I'd set out to do and Forever had pulled out everything he had when I asked him.' In retrospect it was an even better performance because when Sunnyside Up continued his career as St James, he won many big classes with Nick Skelton in the saddle. On this occasion, Forever was a shade faster but St James was to turn the tables on more than one occasion in the ensuing years.

The Sanyo Talent Spotters' Championship, an idea strongly supported by Harvey Smith, was inaugurated to cater for horses who are Grade B at the beginning of the season but who soon find themselves in a competitive void with only the choice of popular opens or classes for more experienced horses in which to jump.

NICK

Nick will never forget winning the Aachen Grand Prix in June 1982, because of the dramatic 'Ride of the Valkyrie' conditions in which he rode his final round and the calibre of the horses that stood below him and the little roan, Everest If Ever. They were: second, Flambeau (Frederic Cottier), France; third, Deister (Paul Schockemohle), Germany; and fourth, Gladstone (Hugo Simon), Austria.

I couldn't believe the weather. Before the class it had rained continuously and the ground was desperately slushy and deep. When I came in for the fourth and final round, the hailstones positively hammered down, stinging my back and If Ever's face, while rain sheeted across the arena. I went like hell, and when, having achieved what proved to be the winning clear, we returned to the collecting ring, it was submerged by an apparent tidal wave of water. The horses were so frightened by the thunder, lightning and dark sky that they were whinnying to each other and If Ever gave a worried neigh.

This was If Ever's first big class after being eliminated in the World Championship at Dublin a couple of weeks earlier. Nick remembers:

I felt very much the underdog before the class. The trouble with

If Ever is that you never know if he will put in a stop although he does this much less now and hopefully the elimination problem is over. He remains a bit difficult to ride to the fences because he's hard to hold and would rather arrange his own strides as we approach a jump. He'll do anything to be awkward and unco-operative.

Three horses were again clear in the final round. The six jumps included an upright by the side of the lake, which was just like a slide, a massive parallel by the dyke, a parallel by a wall and a triple bar to finish. 'When I'd jumped the last parallel, I just loosed him for home and he went as fast as he could go, galloping all the way up to the triple while I sat as tight as possible.'

The enigmatic If Ever was in one of his most compliant moods on a most beneficial occasion. Although he is so unpredictable in competition, Nick says he is 'perfect in the stable. It's the only place where I can do anything with him.'

The Grand Finale, the Aachener Farewell, which followed was a catastrophe with all the horses out of line because they wouldn't go head-first into the terrible storm. Every participating horse and rider was soaked to the skin.

LESLEY

Television commentator David Coleman and his wife Barbara have long been among Ted and Liz's closest friends. One of their daughters, Anne, herself a former British Champion and now married to Devon International Tony Newbery, used to spend much of her time when she was younger at Elms Farm for schooling. So when neither Ted nor Liz was free to travel with Lesley to the Junior European Championships at Aarau, Switzerland, in 1981, because Liz and Nick had a very important show at the same time, Anne was the ideal choice to accompany Lesley because not only was she already a friend, but also she knew the Edgars' methods inside out.

Lesley was very happy with the arrangement, so the pair took One More Time and travelled with fellow competitor Zoe Bates and her parents.

The weather was outstanding when they arrived, but on the

third day, just after Britain had won the Nations' Cup, the heavens opened and it rained and rained, all night long, only stopping at the start of the European Individual Junior Championship. Then as soon as the competition and prize-winners' parade were over, it began to pour with rain again.

Lesley recollects,

Anne was really helpful; just having someone there on whom I could totally rely meant an awful lot. I walked the course on my own, but it was being able to ask questions and be reassured that helped me so much. I found her a marvellous companion too.

There were four of us in the individual final jump-off; the three others were boys, and I was the last to go. The first and second riders from Spain and Holland had four faults and a slow clear respectively. Then, the third rider, Germany's Peter Jostes was clear on Pascal with a slightly faster round. I did not send on One More Time quite as fast as usual, but to my surprise, I won by the margin of over five seconds. As I landed over the last fence with a faultless round, it gave me the most marvellous feeling, the crowd went mad and I was unbelievably happy.

After the presentation, the French and the Dutch teams combined to sling the victor into the water jump: 'I still had my boots and breeches on but at least they took off my jacket first,' recalls Lesley. She was so overwhelmed that she didn't care and managed to pull a couple of her assailants into the water with her. 'I knew Ted was away, but when I managed to escape, the first thing I did was to phone Liz and tell her the news.'

The Radio Rentals Grand Prix at the Horse of the Year Show was another *moment suprême* for Lesley. In the first round Barbarella hit one fence quite hard but other than that the mare was riding exceedingly well. In the second round the bogey fence proved to be a big white vertical off a corner which fell with boring regularity. 'Barbarella picked up much better than I dared hope and met the problem spot-on right.'

In the third round, Barbarella was clear and Ted, who had schooled her that morning, said to Lesley, 'Don't go in and blow your brains. Aim for a nice steady clear.' The young Scots rider Gary Gillespie ran Lesley uncomfortably close on Goldfink, and could, in Lesley's words, 'easily have beaten me'. However, he lost valuable time on the turn to the last, leaving Lesley the victor on Cliff Cox's FMS Barbarella. Gary Gillespie was second, and Hugo Simon third.

Lesley reflects on the celebrations:

It was my first Grand Prix success, so I was desperately excited. On the last night of the Horse of the Year Show, Ted always drives back to Warwickshire, which is far better than waking up in London the next day and wasting the morning driving back home. When we arrived back at Rio Grande, the first thing Ted did was to open a bottle of champagne in my honour. We downed it with a special cake which Liz produced from out of the blue. It was a fantastic feeling, sitting drinking champagne and celebrating until four o'clock in the morning.

SOME DAYS IT ALL GOES WRONG

The combination of a suddenly recalcitrant horse and a totally committed rider have been the contributory factor of some of the most spectacular show-jumping spills. Like all the world's top competitors, the Everest riders have had their share.

Wallaby is a class horse and class usually pays dividends, but there is always the odd exception . . .

FACING PAGE
ABOVE Forever and Liz in full flight at the Horse of the Year Show, 1980. (*Bob Langrish*)

BELOW A proud moment, Liz receives the Queen Elizabeth Cup from Princess Margaret after her victory on Forever, 1979. (*Kit Houghton*)

In a competition at Arena North, the first fence was a big parallel by the side of the permanent lake. Following this the riders could choose between going right-handed and up and down over the bank to a fence on the far side, or left-handed, nipping round by the inside of the lake. Reaching the next fence by the latter route was much the faster proposition.

Nick decided to jump left-handed, go down the bank a little bit and round the short way. Wallaby was not enthusiastic about descending the bank, so Nick kicked him on and he jumped right off the top, straight into the lake. Says Nick,

Wallaby hit the base of the lake, which is made of concrete, and tipped clean over. He finished up upside down with me underneath him, my boots and hat full of water. I was soaked from

top to toe. There was a jeer from the collecting ring as I rode towards it intending to retire, but the riders sent me back, to continue.

Nick jumped the next two fences, then he came to a double of parallels separated by two strides. His saddle was drenched and his breeches were soaking as he approached in a shower of spray. Wallaby jumped the first parallel, died on the next two strides, took off a mile away for the second parallel, dropped his back feet between the poles in a desperate attempt to bank the jump and shot the luckless Nick, who by now had no grip at all because of all the water, clean out of the saddle once again, right over the jump and between Wallaby's ears.

The unfortunate Nick was on the floor for the second time in a matter of minutes to the unsympathetic accompaniment of another big jeer from the collecting ring.

* * *

All members of the Edgar entourage are familiar with 'the white tie saga'. One day, when Ted was still competing, he decided to take three horses to Balsall Common but no one was keen to go with him. However, despite the likelihood of no supporters, he decided to make the trip.

When Ted competed he always liked to be turned out correctly. Liz jokes, 'As I was out shopping, his "valet" wasn't at hand and he couldn't find a white tie. He rummaged around, had to settle for another colour and drove off to the show on his own, in a very bad mood indeed.'

At Balsall Common, matters swiftly took a turn for the worse, Ted was dumped by one of the horses, ripping his best hacking jacket in the process.

He arrived home absolutely furious. When he had cooled down, Liz offered to mend the hole in his jacket, but Ted utterly refused saying crossly, 'I shall live with it to punish you, to remind everyone of my misfortunes.'

* * *

One September, Makedo had jumped inordinately well, eclipsing his rivals at the three-day City of Birmingham Show in Perry Park,

FACING PAGE
ABOVE LEFT A superb jump by Forever over a very big fence in the Grand Prix at Paris in 1981. (*Bob Langrish*)

ABOVE RIGHT Liz and Forever, against the magnificent backcloth of Windsor Castle, one of the world's most attractive settings. (*Bob Langrish*)

BELOW The British squad with their silver medals at the Substitute Olympics at Rotterdam in 1980. From left to right: Tim Grubb, Nick, John Whitaker, Graham Fletcher with their chef d'équipe Ronnie Massarella. (*Bob Langrish*)

Only a video film could explain how Ted managed to regain his seat in Uncle Max's saddle after this seeming disaster during the 1969 Dublin Grand Prix.

so Liz set off for the Wales and West Show the next day with her morale high.

Makedo was established as a course specialist and Liz positively radiated good humour at the prospect of staying with her parents and jumping on the family showground. But, the trials and tribulations of show-jumping are never far away, even from the cream of the riders.

At the double of gates, Liz realised that Makedo had landed too far in. 'Steady!' she called and Makedo obeyed her implicitly:

He slowed down all right. In fact he stopped dead, a stride away from the second gate, and I cleared it all on my own after being shot out of the saddle and soaring forward straight over his head.

*   *   *

At the Royal Dublin Horse Show in 1969, Ted and Uncle Max, the new holders of the King George V Gold Cup, came into the ring for the final Grand Prix jump-off, hopeful of achieving another prestigious victory. With a certain degree of confidence, Ted sent the bucking grey through the start.

In the middle of the combination, there was a gate. Uncle Max jumped in and suddenly swung out left-handed, decanting Ted out of the saddle. With great presence of mind, Ted somehow heaved himself back into the saddle with his right hand, using the pillar of the gate as a support. Uncle Max then successfully negotiated the combination and subsequently the course but his chance of success had evaporated.

*   *   *

When Lesley was still a junior, she rode Shipley Hills in the Pony Derby at Pyecombe, Sussex. The competition was sponsored by the General Chip Company who supply the wood chips that many show-jumpers use for their horses' bedding. Accordingly, the last fence was a set of planks with a big trough of chips underneath. Nick and Ted were standing by this obstacle as Lesley approached, clear up to that moment.

'I'll show them how it's done,' I thought. As I approached, in what I fondly hoped was perfect style, I got everything wrong, missed, and, before I knew it, I found myself lying in a bed of shavings, the Derby lost, and a huge mass of wood chips descending on me from the sky.

*   *   *

CHAPTER SIX

THE EVEREST STUD

In 1977, the Everest Stud numbered ten horses. Six years later, in 1983, the enterprise had exactly doubled with twenty horses.

One of the dominant factors in the continuing success of the Everest Stud horses is attention to detail, no matter how minuscule. It is run in a similar manner to the yard of top National Hunt trainer, Michael Dickinson, who has a reputation for leaving not even a pebble unturned.

At the 1982 Royal International Horse Show, Dickinson shadowed Ted and Liz like a dog for three days, at the end of which he told Ted, 'When I get home, I shall give my jockeys a right roasting when they need one, just like you!'

Another contributory reason is the staff, and those who worked through the winter of 1982/83 and in 1983 were all top class. They were: grooms Lisa and Susie, and nanny Julie, who is an absolute rock. The plain fact is that if staff don't work and cannot be trusted one hundred per cent, whether Ted and Liz are there or not, the wins will not come regularly.

All in all, involvement in the Everest Stud means being part of a concerted team effort, and David Kingsley is very much part of the team. He has become a patron of show-jumping as well as a partner and friend to Ted and Liz. He also makes matters easy for them by allowing them to take their own decisions and by understanding that there are bad days as well as good.

Ted will never forget buying a horse for £20,000 and almost immediately receiving an offer of £30,000. When the horse had been at Elms Farm for only a few days, he tripped over and broke his neck. When Ted rang David to tell him, David's reply was not 'That's bad luck,' but 'Don't worry, we've got plenty more horses and we'll buy others.' According to Ted, 'He's a real friend; he'd never turn round and criticise us.'

Another peripheral member of the set-up is public relations expert, Jean Kittermaster, whose company handles the Everest Stud's publicity. Apart from her sharp business acumen, the fact that Jean herself is an accomplished horsewoman is an immense asset.

Placing the horses is an art. Starting the top horses only in classes that they have a reasonable chance of winning includes realistically assessing their abilities and not wearing rose-coloured spectacles. 'Keep yourself in the best company and your horses in the worst,' is a saying that Liz and Ted try to put into practice.

Discipline is essential for success with horses and Liz keeps a tight watch for thoroughness throughout the Stud. When she goes out into the stables, she never hesitates to point out something which is not being done correctly. Those who work at the Stud are well aware that if they don't like their particular job, they can, as Ted maintains, 'Walk down the road. There are plenty more fish in the sea.'

The Everest riders all have their whims and ways, and Ted

The corral-style paddocks at Rio Grande. From left to right: Radius, Carat and Forever. (*Bob Langrish*)

makes it a priority to know their worries, because, without this knowledge, he cannot help them. 'Nick gets a bit edgy before a class – it's his way; but if you're going to give your best, you have to get keyed up ... and my riders are in to win. There's a great saying: "Winning is something, losing is nothing".'

Pre- and post-competition tension is inevitable in all forms of physical activity. I remember sitting next to Margot Fonteyn and Rudolf Nureyev in a London restaurant after they had given a stunning performance in *Swan Lake* at The Royal Opera House, Covent Garden. It was a full hour before they could relax and talk to each other. Yet sometimes inexperienced equestrian reporters accuse a rider of being unco-operative because he does not wish to talk to them in depth immediately before or during a class; this is a totally unreasonable request.

A TYPICAL DAY

A typical day at Rio Grande begins at 6.30 a.m. Ted is usually awake; Liz is woken by the Teasmade. The grooms, Lisa and Susie, are in the stables no later than 6.45 a.m. beginning the feeding, and Nick, who has woken at 6.30 a.m., arrives soon after having driven the three miles from his home. Ted is in the stables by 7 a.m. The feeding is worked out by Ted and Liz with the aim of keeping the horses sensible. Their finesse in this department is illustrated by the continuing well-being of the Everest horses – their coats always shine. Their expertise is evident because they can keep a horse going for a long time without it going 'over the top'. Individual attention is essential to cater for a sluggish horse who needs more oats or a hard-to-feed gassy horse who needs calming.

Nick usually feeds his own horses and by 8 a.m. sharp the feeding and mucking out is completed. When they are at Rio Grande, Ted and Nick do the morning mucking out, driving a tractor and cart straight down the central passageway. Ted, Nick and Liz sit down to the breakfast that Liz has prepared as nanny Julie leaves to take Marie, who likes to arrive early at school, probably to buy extra sweets for the day at a nearby tuck-shop.

The conversation revolves round plans for the day, which Liz usually writes out as they decide together what will be best for each horse. On Wednesday, 23rd February, 1983, as Liz could not ride her usual horses (due to a knee injury incurred a few days earlier) and as Ted was going to be away a few days, the pattern was irregular. More often than not everyone, including Lisa, Susie and Julie, rides at least one horse and other horses are worked loose in the school.

Julie arrives back from taking Marie to school, helps clear the table and washes up as Ted makes two phone calls. They are to order some tendon and fetlock boots and to see if David Tatlow is bringing a horse over that morning. By 8.30 a.m. the team set out to start the exercising and write the names of the horses going to the show in the afternoon in chalk on the black brick square opposite the tack room.

The next day Ted is flying out to Florida to try and buy a horse he saw at the World Championship in Dublin the previous June, and he won't be home before Nick's horses leave for the World Cup Qualifier at Antwerp. Nick asks Ted to give If Ever a school for him so Ted puts on two anoraks and his cap (it is −8° outside) and sets off.

He hacks down the road across the farm to a large flat field alongside a motorway bank which helps keep some of the frost out of the ground. If Ever is soon doing some faster work. He must be ready to compete in little over a week. Short-striding, he is cantered sharply round the perimeter of the field and as the steam starts to rise, Ted takes off the horse's work sheet.

Ted begins to make more serious demands from If Ever, including shoulder-in and half-pass. After almost an hour's concentrated work, Ted hacks home, and If Ever, who is remarkably small for a horse with such a phenomenal jump, relaxes as he is hosed down in the wash box to remove the sweat from his steaming roan coat.

While Ted was out and Nick was working 'Woody' (Everest Radius) in the school, Nick's wife Sarah drove their box over to Rio Grande bringing her horse, Sherwood, for a work-out and also to continue breaking in a young mare. Two days earlier the mare ran havoc in the indoor school, galloping up and then along the hay bales at the far end, denting the aluminium wall before landing back-first in a crevice.

In a furore of activity, bales were moved and a rope thrown round the mare who was dragged out on her back to the arena biting and lashing out in front throughout. 'A good horse would

Loose schooling If Ever. (*Bob Langrish*)

have been knocked to bits,' Ted commented, 'but all the mare did
was lose a little hair round her groin.'

Thirty-six hours later, the mare has capitulated and is co-oper-
ating all she can with Sarah who is working her bareback, with
only a roller and foam-rubber pad. The mare, who has a silky
mouth, has dropped her head and is producing an amazingly
cadenced trot, really moving both in front and behind. Sarah has
triumphed but Ted counsels Nick, 'There are plenty of horses
needing breaking; Sarah doesn't have to have the rough ones.'

For safety reasons, no one is allowed to work a horse on his or
her own in the school unless there is someone watching.

At eleven o'clock, Nick, Liz, Sarah and Ted come into the
kitchen for a quick cup of coffee, then they all go out to loose-
school a chestnut novice indoors. Ted has a whip to crack to keep

the horse's attention and ensure that he is onward bound. Everyone helps see that the horse makes full use of the corners and the jump is altered as necessary. It is gradually changed and the placing pole adjusted to help the inexperienced horse take off in the right place. This is concentrated work for a young horse and under half an hour is quite enough. The horse is taken away to be washed and dried off.

As a general rule, when Ted and Liz first school a young horse, it is not given too long a period of concentrated work, perhaps only fifteen minutes ridden work in the covered school, then probably hacked out. They try to vary the work pattern. Another day, the horse might run loose in the school.

Ted explains,

> We all work together if I'm loose-schooling a horse; I may need someone to help me. If any horse is going to jump, everyone is there to see. You just can't keep them away. Mention 'jump' and they are all there up by the fences.

Every day, Ted rides some of the horses and he watches all those whose schedule includes a jump. Each week, Ted probably sits on every horse at least once. Liz says,

> Whatever Ted does, the horses all jump better when he's ridden them. Forever has always been such a gentleman to me that he has not needed very much schooling; Ted has hardly ridden him. But every success I had with Wallaby was always entirely due to Ted. Now he rides Nick's horses for Nick too and after each time they improve.

Great stress is laid on stride, so that after concentrated schooling, a horse's stride can be lengthened or shortened at the push of a button, rather like putting a little pressure on the accelerator of a Ferrari. This means the horse should meet the fence at the perfect distance and if it has sufficient scope, arrive at the right speed, leaving the jump standing.

Lack of stride has produced some terrible falls over fixed fences in the eventing world. Even in National Hunt racing, stride matters now. In old racing pictures, the jockeys can be seen sitting right back, riding on a wing and a prayer, either booting on or utterly oblivious of the situation. Now the best jockeys, like Johnny Francome, ride a hole or two longer than they used to, sitting forward and picking their stride whenever possible.

By 12.45 p.m. all the horses have been worked and lunch is being prepared in the kitchen by Julie and Liz. Lol Weaver arrives. He always comes for lunch on Wednesdays. The meal usually includes the family favourite, a Caesar Salad with croûtons, which Ted and Liz learnt to enjoy in the States, and always a selection of cold meats, maybe a pork pie or scotch eggs and also bread, butter and cheese. There

August 1983 – Nick gives St James his first jump after his accident at the Royal International. (*Bob Langrish*)

is an assortment of mayonnaise, avocado dressing, chutney and pickles. Everyone helps themselves and if it is a cold day, there is soup for anyone who would like a bowl. Afterwards everyone has coffee.

Ted, Liz and Nick are all going to a show at Balsall Common with the horses which will be ridden by Liz and Nick. Liz phones through to the show to talk to either Jean Sillett or Sheila Billingham, formerly the Harper sisters, who now run the Balsall Common Arena which their father Albert founded, to find out how far the show-jumping classes have progressed. The competitions at this winter series of shows are very popular and well filled. As well as local riders of all degrees of experience, others, such as John Whitaker, consider it well worth while coming down from Yorkshire to school their novices.

Liz announces that they should leave at 3.30 p.m. and everyone involved goes their separate ways to prepare. Nick goes to tell Lisa and Susie the time the horses need to be loaded for departure.

Forever about to hit the road. (*Bob Langrish*)

As this was a local show Liz estimated they would return after competing by 7.30 p.m. Before Liz went and collected her regulation breeches, boots, hat and tweed jacket, as this is a small informal occasion, she prepared supper which Julie will put in the oven while she is away. It is to be roast beef, one of Ted's favourites, and a huge haunch of beef is put into the baking pan. Liz cleaned a mass of spring greens and peeled some potatoes ready to roast. There will be eight for supper, including Lisa and Susie, who have been invited to join the family.

On a more usual winter day without a show at which to compete, Liz usually spends the afternoon doing a variety of jobs in the house or doing some essential shopping before preparing supper. Ted attends to the farm and talks to his farm manager, while Nick might alter the jumps in the field in front of the house, help turn out a tack room, harrow the indoor school or clean out a lorry. Lisa and Susie polish the tack and feed the horses. The aim is to finish all the work by 5 p.m. One of the girls always goes out at 9 or 10 p.m. to check all is well in the stables before going to bed.

On normal days Ted and Liz are at hand to help or advise with schooling etc. and generally keep an eye on proceedings. They are constantly in and out of the stables, checking food supplies, the date of the horses' regular worm-dose, or to collect a piece of broken tack or a torn rug that will be picked up and mended in the minimum time by their friend Geoff Charley who owns Townfield Saddlers. Luckily he almost passes their door every night on the way home from his business.

THE STABLES

Ted is one hundred per cent Western orientated. 'He'd love to be a swinging, long-striding cowboy,' appreciates Liz. 'If he were born again, it would undoubtedly be out in the States and he would probably arrive wearing a big Stetson hat into the bargain.'

When the Edgars realised they had outgrown Ponderosa, Ted conceived the idea of Rio Grande and its superb accompanying stable complex, a virtual palace for horses, to which the inmates of the Everest Stud moved in September 1982. Rio Grande incorpor-

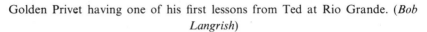

Golden Privet having one of his first lessons from Ted at Rio Grande. (*Bob Langrish*)

ates all the good ideas Ted has seen during his travels throughout North America, the Antipodes and Europe.

The new set-up was built on a four-acre parcel of land which the Edgars owned, at the south end of Elms Farm towards Leamington on the other side of Leek Wootton from the Warwick by-pass. The Edgars did not really want to leave Leek Wootton because the 200 acres they farm is first-class land and the situation, being close to the centre of the national motorway grid, is ideal for travelling to shows.

Keith Cockell's original assignment was to build a ranch-type bungalow resembling those dotted all over Texas and Florida, with a big sweeping roof and a verandah all round, faced with wood and exposed 'cowboy-style' bricks. The adjacent stable block was to be in American barn style and co-ordinate with the house.

Keith is managing director of a Leek Wootton building company specialising in producing houses for those wanting something far from run of the mill. He is also a designer for the Talbot Car Company.

When the plans were drawn up, he worked very closely throughout with Ted and foreman Dave Matthews as the two deep-red buildings mushroomed out of the soil on the far side of Ted's farm, where eleven houses, each with a paddock or access to one, are currently being built.

Visitors entering under the typical ranch-style arch and passing up the drive will see the stables on the left and the house on the right, towards the top of a gentle rise. The total stable complex is 200 × 150 feet and all the necessities are under cover, with no need for the horses to step out and face the elements at any time.

From outside, the huge building appears much more elaborate than originally envisaged, because the planning authorities refused permission for a cheap asbestos roof, so the roofing material is traditional red pantiles to match the house. Like the house, the walls are a combination of red-stained pine and exposed bricks.

Ted's request was for twenty stables and a farm shed which could double for use as an indoor school. This measures 120 × 60 feet and is in the centre of the building.

It has aluminium walls and six lines of translucent skylights in the roof. The base is packed dirt with muck on top, then very deep shavings. The shed houses all the hay, as well as providing a schooling area for the horses.

Ted describes his thinking behind the accommodation:

> I've always thought that however many boxes you have, you always fill 'em. If you have forty boxes, you'll have twenty bad horses. Even among the twenty horses we have now there are some who shouldn't be here.
>
> There aren't twenty good jumpers anywhere under one roof, and I can't bear to feed rubbish. If a horse isn't any good, I wouldn't even take it to a show.

The stable area comprises boxes each measuring 14×12 feet in two long lines facing each other, American barn style, with a wide central passageway. They were largely constructed out of breeze blocks for economy and also because this eliminates the possibility of chewing through boredom.

At work in the school. From left to right: Pip Lyons, Marie Edgar and Julie Salt. (*Bob Langrish*)

The floors are of packed dirt and the wet just sinks away as the ground is relatively high. Ted does not like concrete floors. 'It'd be like making a person stand continually on a stone floor instead of a carpet. Concrete is bad for horses' feet and legs.'

Ted prefers straw, but the horses are all on deep shavings because he has found this greatly reduces leg trouble. The mangers are surmounted by oval, brick-lined apertures, so the girl grooms can save time by walking straight down the line and feeding the horses without going into the boxes.

The mangers are divided into sections, one for hard food and the other for hay.

The doors are of wire netting so that it is easy to see at once if a horse has lost his rugs or bandages, or if he is out of sorts. 'Most horses spend at least twenty hours a day caged in their boxes and boarded up, often unable to see each other,' says Ted. 'Our horses can see everything that's going on.'

On a fine day they can look across the sheep-filled fields of the farm to Leek Wootton because, on the outside walls, the stables have loose-box style top doors which can be opened and pegged back from outside, letting in fresh air and sunshine.

All the work on the horses is done outside the boxes in the central aisle, with the horses secured by pillar reins of metal chain, to a ring on each side of the passageway, as is a common practice in the States. Here they are groomed and have their feet picked out, then they are taken to the big box close by the entrance to be saddled up. This box is also used for clipping and washing down.

The long feed room comprises a row of metal-lidded bins which are one hundred per cent vermin-proof. Three carpeted adjoining rooms are devoted to caring for and storing tack. The first is a utility working room, with two washing machines for cleaning rugs and bandages and also the grooms' clothes. The second houses the everyday tack, and the third the show tack and rugs. Further down the corridor are two boxes where Marie keeps her ponies.

On the far side of the farm shed lies a long storage shed, measuring 120 × 40 feet. It is open at one end and is the only area Ted has to store his farm machinery. Penned in at the closed end are three Charollais cattle from which he hopes to build up a high-class herd, watched over by a guard of lavender and grey guinea-fowl and bantams.

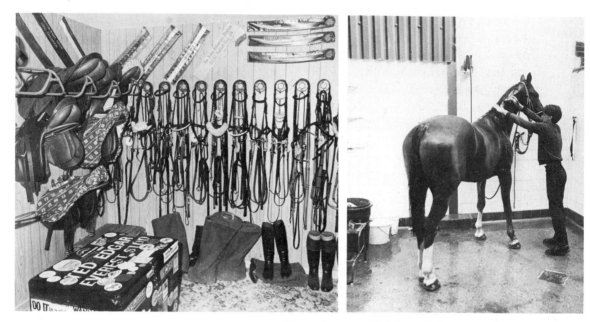

ABOVE LEFT The tack room. (*Bob Langrish*)

ABOVE RIGHT Shower time for Flame, seen here with Pip Lyons. (*Bob Langrish*)

Two separate staircases lead up to six bedrooms, two shower rooms, two kitchens and two living rooms for grooms, which are over the tack rooms. This area is ideally situated for all involved to maintain the closest possible surveillance over their charges.

BUYING HORSES

Ted is ninety-nine per cent in charge of the crucial buying and selling of horses. He thinks that riders are seldom the best judges of horses and elaborates:

For me, Nick is among the world's most brilliant jockeys, but one of the worst men to take anywhere to buy anything because he makes them all look like Grand Prix material. One mare he recommended is now out in the field in foal. Buying is my job.

Nick suggested Ted consider a horse he'd seen in Australia that was 'out of this world'. So Ted flew out specially in February 1983, but did not buy the horse even though it was good because he did not think it would adapt to English courses. He recalls, 'I'm not running him down in any way but it takes years of experience, and even now I know I can make mistakes all too easily.' Now, Ted would never ever ask Nick to ride a horse he was considering buying because Nick would get the very best out of the horse rather than reveal its natural ability.

'I always seem to be much luckier when I go buying on my own, make up my own mind and stand on my own judgement.' When he goes to see a horse, and what he asks to see it do, all depend on which country he is in. In the winter of 1983 he bought a horse at 6 o'clock in the morning:

> I'd travelled five hundred miles the previous day looking at horses. At 2 a.m. I was taken into a school, feeling cold, wet and miserable; it was $-6°$. The horse was brought out, and I thought, 'Oh, my Christ, I wish you'd jump, because you're such a good-looking horse,' for never yet have I seen a good-looking horse really jump. But could it jump, so I stayed up until 5 a.m. to do a deal.'

That horse was Halo who won two classes at his first English outdoor shows in April 1983: at the Heythrop Hunt Show near Chipping Norton and the Gate Inn near Coleshill on consecutive days.

People often ring up Ted to tell him they have seen a good horse he should buy, but usually when he follows up such information, it proves fruitless. 'Such a mission has only worked once, with Boomerang.' When Ted arrived to see him he was awkward to ride but his jump was fantastic. 'He couldn't even change his hind legs; he had no mouth.'

'Usually I fall over, run into or bump into horses; horses I shouldn't and wouldn't have seen but by chance, perhaps in some-one's back garden.' One of the greatest, 'really honest' horses in Ted's book is Jet Lag. Ted bought him from David Tatlow for a hunter price, £2,000, for a local lady MFH to hunt. That was in 1977. When Ted went to help Liz in the States, the lady MFH sent him back because he was wrong in the wind. Sometime after Ted arrived home from America he was riding back across the jumping field and decided to give Jet Lag a jump. The only fence standing was a 4 feet 9 inch vertical, and, before Liz could lower the fence, he had jumped it clear in both directions. He was immediately promoted from hunter to jumper.

Developing a promising show-jumper into an international requires time, patience and the knowledge to put in the specialised groundwork. Taking things slowly, waiting two or three years if necessary, and jumping as many clears as possible, are all part of Ted's philosophy and practice when educating young horses:

> At first horses seldom listen to you. They must learn to stop, start, walk, canter, trot, twist, turn, lengthen and shorten. Our method is a mile away from pure dressage, but it is a form of dressage. Former international Anneli Wucherpfennig [née Drummond-Hay], who now lives in South Africa, summed it up the right way when she said, 'You do dressage with show-jumping in mind.'

Having found the right material, it cannot be over-emphasised that without the right rider the entire effort is a waste of time. One of the Everest Stud's major assets is that Liz and Nick are two of the world's greatest jockeys. A million pounds won't make a jockey, the essential quality is the gift of being a natural horseman.

When looking to buy, Ted reckons,

> You don't want all those foreigners. You're much better off with an Irish horse, if you can find one. Every German, Dutch or Belgian horse I've ever had, you can hammer with work, dressage-wise, and they love it, but no Irish horse would take that. Ten minutes schooling with them and you're away over the jumps.

Tommy Brennan rang Ted one morning at 6 o'clock and said, 'By Jesus, you have to get out of the bed! I've a horse here that's very good, but it's a bit difficult. Would you be interested?' Ted caught the next plane and arrived at Dublin Horse Show at 10.30 a.m. and had the horse out straight away: 'Eddie Macken rode him and I had him bought at 10.45 a.m. The horse was due to jump in a class at 12 o'clock with Eddie on board, and the conditions of the sale were that if he won the competition, there would be no deal, because he would not be eligible for the English Foxhunter Classes.' Luckily, he had a fence down, so he was still a Foxhunter. Ted bought him and travelled him straight back home. This horse was the immortal Boomerang.

Ted bought Boomerang for himself because he was so difficult. However, Liz got on him two days later, and the following Saturday she won on him at a show. 'I never did get the ride on him,' Ted remembers with an affectionate smile. Boomerang cost Ted £3,500.

1972 was a good year for jumpers at the Royal Dublin Show. Ted bought the black Himself from an undertaker and also had a chance to buy Heatwave who was later snapped up by David Broome.

Although Ted prefers Irish horses and regularly combs Ireland, in the last four years he has only bought one, Domino, because he can hardly ever find the right type. On the rare occasion he has, the price has usually been extortionate. Ted saw Domino at the Millstreet Derby Meeting in 1982 and bought him within an hour of seeing him jump. It proved difficult to get Domino home. Not only did his owner live in Northern Ireland, in trouble-ridden Derry, but he almost changed his mind as he hadn't really wanted to sell the horse, so Ted had to enlist the help of his friend Con Power, who lives near Dublin, to collect the horse.

Although a high percentage of the horses Ted buys live up to his expectations, there are inevitably a few who, for a variety of reasons, fail to make the grade and are not worth perseverance. Feeding and schooling horses costs money and a bad horse costs as much to keep as a good one. Ted and Liz's ability to realise at a relatively early stage that a horse does not have all the qualities they demand, and sell the horse on, contributes to their success.

They are in search of potential internationals and the horses they sell have a first-class basic training. These horses are in demand, and regularly win, when sold to owners who buy them with the national circuit or young riders' classes in mind.

CHAPTER SEVEN

HOME

The Rio Grande is designed 'par excellence' for a horse-orientated life. Ted always had the idea of an 'A' line roof 'with a verandah and bit of a skirt to it'. He started off with that and the rest followed. 'Visitors from Australia say it's a typical Aussie house,' says Liz, 'and those from the States say it's American. Ted likes to think it's cowboy-style.'

Inside the house the entrance leads into the huge high kitchen where full advantage is taken of the A-shaped roof, giving an attractive barn-shaped interior. It is the only room where the full available space has been used, all the others have flat ceilings, so there is masses of loft or future bedroom space available.

The kitchen measures twenty-seven by fifteen feet with windows on two sides. One, a set of French windows, faces the stables and outside there is room for Ted to sit on the verandah in his rocking chair on a hot summer's night. The other is at the front of the house, overlooking a newly levelled field with its permanent bank and ditches.

Liz designed the comprehensive kitchen which includes a square, red-tiled cooking area. It incorporates a matching oil-powered Aga and sink, and oak storage cupboards. It is invariably spotless. At the far end there is a long table and chairs, close to the French windows. 'Everyone comes through the door into the kitchen,' Liz explains. 'It is the room where we eat, relax and spend a great deal of our time indoors.'

Running off the kitchen are a boot room and cloakroom on one side and a utility room on the other. Further along is a larder, behind which is Liz's office.

The dining room is next to the kitchen, off the hall with its permanent bar, then the open-plan lounge and long passage through to the bedroom area.

Marie's room has a bathroom which interlinks with a guest room. There are also two smaller bedrooms with a shower-room between them. Ted and Liz's room has an adjacent bathroom with jacuzzi.

A circular staircase down from the hall past a brick wall leads to the front door, which, one suspects, will seldom be opened. Alongside, there is a cloakroom with a really neat minuscule handbasin.

Under the stairs in a low cool position, there is a wine cupboard. Here is also a large laundry room with extensive drying facilities, both hanging and automatic. This has a separate external door so the grooms can go in and out without disturbing visitors in the kitchen.

The swimming pool from Ponderosa has been re-sited at the back of Rio Grande and landscaped with roses and lawns. It is reached from a hall leading from the garage; eventually it will be covered. At Ponderosa the pool was used by Marie and Ted as Liz cannot swim, although her holidays are more often than not spent in some exotic hot country, where she prefers to relax in the heat

The Rio Grande. (*Bob Langrish*)

by a pool, as opposed to sight seeing. This is a situation she now plans to rectify, despite an unnerving experience watching the movie 'Jaws II', after which Marie comforted, 'Don't worry, the shark wouldn't fit in our pool.'

It is utterly daunting for a less well-organised person to observe the efficient ease with which Liz combines the roles of housewife, wife, mother and secretary, while remaining a top international show-jumper.

Despite the continual comings and goings from the stables, and the fact that Liz's two corgis, the black Bessie and small champagne-coloured Sherry, follow her everywhere, the house is never less than immaculate, a situation which Liz attributes to her help, Lesley Semple, who comes on her bicycle every morning and cleans for two hours as she did at Ponderosa.

The shopping is another of Liz's chores. She gets the basic necessities at a cash and carry in Warwick which is two miles away. Originally she went once every six weeks, but now that the complex has mushroomed and she has so many more to feed she usually has to go once a fortnight.

In the house during the winter of 1982/83, when there was not a show at which to compete, she catered for five at every meal: herself and Ted, Marie, nanny Julie, and Lesley who always had all her meals with them and lived much as an elder daughter. Nick has breakfast and lunch every day and sometimes Sarah, his wife, comes over too. Liz also buys for the girl grooms of whom there are never less than two, often three, and there are usually more mouths to feed at weekends. She often cooks for the grooms, and always tries to include them when she does a roast or when they have been to a show.

Catering becomes more complicated in the show season when food also has to be provided in the horse-box for those away at shows overnight. Then she cooks in the lorry when the classes are over and horses are comfortably settled, or, if the weather is good, may barbecue outside, although 'we have been known to barbecue in the rain'. Just before leaving to drive the box down to the Royal Bath and West in June 1983, she was combining packing her clothes with cooking a delicious-looking chicken concoction to warm up in the horse-box cooker that night.

Inevitably, there is a continual mountain of washing but with two automatic washing machines and help from Julie, who irons to perfection, Liz says,

> It's not a chore at all. When we get home from a show I put all the breeches and shirts to soak overnight. The next morning they go into the washing machine, then out on the line and the job is done. I quite enjoy ironing and always do some if I have time. I never let a white shirt go to a show unless it's been ironed, not on anyone, it's an absolute law. Everyone must be spotless and well turned out at shows.

Ted and Liz's secretary, Barbara Rushton, who has worked for Ted's family for twenty-five years and who has a first-class knowledge of tax, comes in one night a week to deal with the wages, official and farm paperwork, and everything that needs her special knowledge. Liz copes with all the horse paperwork including the show-jumping entries which are extensive, and includes a totally different group of shows for Marie. This work comes in spasms with much less in November and December because there are no major shows in January and February. But in January each year, she plans for the forthcoming season and enters for the Newark and Nottinghamshire County which is in May.

Liz does this in her office, explaining,

> I am more likely to achieve this in the evening than any other time. I might have to enter ten shows at once and must keep up to date with all the schedules so that I am continually aware of the closing dates for entries. I suppose I do some office work every day. If there is a lot I will sit up till midnight to get it finished. It doesn't worry me too much.

As Marie gets older, Liz is able to enjoy more time with her daughter and says, 'She is very much a friend to me now. She helps with everything, comes around with us increasingly often and I try to be with her as much as possible.'

Marie is taken daily to the Kingsley School in Leamington by Julie and, as an only child, is both self-sufficient and grown up for her age. Most nights when Ted, Liz and Marie are at home together, they play cards. 'She's very clued up, too,' Liz laughs.

Marie could not have a better mentor than Liz to help her with her ponies. When Marie was born, Liz's father Fred bought a two-year-old Welsh pony gelding from the mountains, had it broken in, ridden and shown by a small child. He gave it to Marie when she was two years old. The pony, Jewel, as the 11.2 h.h. chestnut pony is called, has proved a totally smashing mount for Marie.

'From an early age she played with Jewel, bandaged him, tidied him, washed him and led him about, everything you could think of she did with him,' Liz remembers. Riding was not her main interest with the pony, looking after him and caring for him came first. Gradually she acquired confidence to ride him, experimenting in her own time and progressing to a little trot, then a canter and jump:

When she was four years old, we had a very good nanny called Sue who later got married and emigrated to Canada. She kept a horse with us and took Marie for rides round the fields, encouraging her. Sue got her going more than we ever had time to do. Sometimes we took both Marie and Jewel to shows where we were competing and they pottered round the showground.

When I came back from competing in the States in November 1977, and Marie was nearly seven years old, I went to Stoneleigh and saw a pony jumping that I'd seen twelve months earlier and loved the way it jumped. The girl who rode the pony was almost twelve years old and going to be out of 12.2 h.h. classes, so we managed to buy the pony, Bali, that afternoon.

Marie started to jump Bali and went well on him straight away, then in January, Liz and Ted were able to buy Franco, another pony they had seen and liked some six months previously. After Marie's seventh birthday, in February 1978, they went to all the little shows with the two ponies who, Liz recalls, 'were angels and went like bombs'. They hardly went to a show where Marie wasn't

ABOVE Liz working out the entries. (*Bob Langrish*)

BELOW Just back from exercise, Liz (Wallaby) and Marie (Jewel) discussing bridles.

in the money with one of them; the ponies gave her confidence and she became really, really keen.

Marie is tall for her age. She was already growing very fast when she had Bali and soon outgrew him because he was a small pony. He was sold and replaced by another 12.2 h.h. pony, Dunmouse, who was later sold on to the great Brazilian rider, Nelson Pessoa, for his son Rodrigo. Marie continued to grow out of her ponies and at the Hull Show in August 1980, Liz saw a skewbald pony jumping and 'fell for her, hook, line and sinker'. Liz came home, told Ted and they went and saw Mrs Birtwhistle near Harrogate and bought Flicka. Flicka, the 13.2 h.h. pony Marie rode from 1980 through 1983, proved a really great pony.

It would be far too easy to assume that as the daughter of leading internationals and with all the advantages of having her ponies kept in high-class professional show-jumping stables, Marie would be courageous about jumping from the very start, but this was not the case. Despite her daughter's enormous mass of rosettes, Liz assessed in 1983, 'She's still not brave.' I can remember watching Marie have a particularly difficult time on a rather wild pony that was on approval, and wisely not bought although full of jumping ability, in the indoor school at Elms Farm.

'She's getting better now, so long as we give her time and let her do it quietly on her own. If we rush her at all or start to pressurise her, she gives up.' Marie went cubbing and hunting once or twice in the 1982/83 season on Sandown Rowan, a local 13.2 h.h. pony, who jumps so very well indoors and was bought to replace Franco. Sandown Rowan was later sold on to Rodrigo Pessoa.

After getting her initial confidence from her nanny Sue, Marie has picked up most of what she knows by watching and listening. She spends much of her time observing Nick and her mother and father school the horses and then experiments herself. Liz considers,

Marie tries out ideas that are far too advanced for her years. It is probably this that has made her a bit scarey. She is not capable of doing things we do, but she thinks she should be able to. Rather than keeping her jumping on a low profile and enjoying it, which is what I hope she will do, she tries to be a professional. She's really set on strides and considering what type of stride she should have approaching a fence. How many thirteen-year-olds would think of that? She just makes life too difficult for herself, whereas her ponies are quite good enough to sort out her problems for her.

When Marie schools her ponies, there is always someone with her. If she needs intensive training, Ted is there; he takes over when everyone else fails. But Nick and Liz give her a lot of help.

Marie would not be her father's daughter if she did not show a degree of spirit, as revealed by the fact she is really naughty in class at school, which she does not like. Liz is strict with Marie with the result that one of the few people Marie respects is her mother. If Liz comes down on Marie, she does what she is told with no come-back. Ted is lenient with his daughter ninety per cent of the time, but she gets a big shock when occasionally she goes a step too far and he descends on her like a ton of bricks.

Liz considers, 'She ought to go to boarding school because then she'd have to behave. Sometimes, probably too feebly, we threaten "September boarding school" if she is naughty.'

Whenever time permits, Liz goes to shows with her daughter, and generally anyone else who is at Rio Grande likes to come too: 'Marie is a right little mine of information when we arrive on the showground. She knows the whole procedure and can carry out everything on her own, which is just as well for all those who have come to help her.'

At the little shows where she most usually competes, Marie first goes and enters, finds out the time of the class and soon sums up the strength of the opposition. The next item on the agenda is to go back to the horse-box and get her pony ready. Liz describes, 'Then madam gets herself ready. She likes to look smart and is always complaining if something doesn't look right, pressing for a new coat, boots or cap. Next she rides-in her pony.'

The following step is to walk the course. At first Liz used to walk with Marie, but now she does not do this because Ted thinks she makes Marie too technical. So, presently, Marie comes out, tells her mother how many yards there are between each fence and asks how many strides she should take.

I used to tell her every stride to take when she was in 12.2 h.h.

classes, whether to hold her pony or kick him on, and she did
what I said like a lamb and often won. But Ted says it's my fault
if she makes a mistake – that's not fair, is it? Now she walks the
course on her own and I try to translate the distances into strides
for her. She generally rides on an extra stride and is not one to
go kicking and blasting down between two fences. Her policy is,
if in doubt have a pull, but she doesn't get into too much trouble
and Flicka is such a good pony.

Marie does not mind if she is not first and is well used to not
winning, although she is often placed. This is because she has
always had very safe ponies which means forfeiting speed to some
degree. In her short show-jumping career she has won some good
classes, but has been second and third much more frequently.
What a pity it is that more show-jumping mothers do not share
Liz's philosophy: 'So long as her ponies have gone well and she's
ridden them well, she's happy and that's how it should be. When
she wins it's a real bonus.'

Liz's days at home begin by producing breakfast at 8 o'clock sharp
for Ted, Marie, Julie and Nick. Breakfast is usually cereals, boiled
or poached eggs and toast. 'Seldom a major cooked breakfast; that
would be a treat.'

The food Liz cooks is basically plain, wholesome and straight-
forward. 'When I cook I'm really cooking what Ted likes, and he
enjoys simple food, no rich sauces. If we're eating out in a restaurant and he arrives late, I can always order for him and get it
right: a sirloin steak, well done.'

By 8.45 a.m. she is out schooling her horses which often takes
all morning. Occasionally if she has a lot to do she does not ride at
all, but that tends to be the exception rather than the rule: 'If
Forever is in I always try to ride him, every day. I don't want to let
that slip or I would lose him. I've never let there be a chance for
anyone else to ride him.'

During the winter of 1982/83 while Forever rested she spent
each morning concentrating on schooling two youngsters, Domino
and a Belgian chestnut that was soon sold on.

The Irish-bred, six-year-old Domino was second in the Boomerang Finder Trial, the equivalent of the British Foxhunter Final,

at Millstreet, County Cork, Ireland, in August 1982 and is a bay gelding by Smooth Stepper out of an unknown, probably part-draught mare. In May 1983, the Earl of Inchcape bought him and he became Nick's ride. A late developer, he may well prove to have the ability to finish up a star.

On the other hand, the rich chestnut-coloured, Belgian six-year-old boasted an impeccable show-jumping pedigree and possessed an immensely kind open eye, which is more often than not the key to a horse's character. His dam was by Furioso, the grandsire of Forever, while his sire is Flugal, who also sired Gay Luron, the horse who carried François Mathy to the bronze Olympic medal at the Montreal Olympics at Bromont in 1976. While his illustrious antecedents suggested a star in the making, his performance belied his breeding.

Liz buys most of her clothes in Leamington Spa, which is only three miles away and has some good shops, or perhaps Stratford-on-Avon, which is useful for dresses. She likes smart clothes for special occasions and has some which last for years. At home she does not have either time or desire to go out shopping and spend lots of money extravagantly, but goes out when she needs something. When jumping abroad in towns like Aachen or Paris where shopping possibilities are vast and the clothes enticing, she would love to explore, but there is seldom time to get near an open shop when she is competing.

Even at home, Liz is always immaculately turned out, usually in cords and sweater which are comfortable and best for darting in and out of the stables during the day. Dressing up for a party is different. 'I reckon it is good for me,' she says, 'and I enjoy the rare occasions when I have sufficient time to do my nails well and really make the effort.'

CHAPTER EIGHT

VIEWS ON THE CONTEMPORARY SCENE

DE-NERVING AND BUTE

The FEI and various National Committees have probably spent more hours over the past few years analysing and trying to assemble their views on the use of the drug 'bute' (Butazolodine) than any other topic. It is a certain bet that heated discussions will continue to take place in the future.

Ted does not want to dope or 'bump and bang horses', but he considers that everyone has to be realistic about show-jumping in the eighties. After all, the sport is changing and developing all the time at an inordinately high speed.

De-nerving is one viable alternative to the use of bute or other drugs to relieve or mask pain. Liz totally agrees that de-nerving is far better than filling up a horse with bute, or putting it down. The Germans have used this method with a great deal of success over the years. Many English enthusiasts would be surprised to know which well-known Hanoverians have undergone this operation.

De-nerving is carried out to allow horses who have become 'footy' with navicular, or who are in the early stages of the onset of the disease, to continue jumping. The most common neurectomy carried out is of the posterior digital nerves which run alongside the flexor tendons at the back of the pastern. It consists of removing a portion of both medial and lateral branches of the nerve. The effect is to remove sensation from the posterior part of the foot, but to leave feeling in the toe.

In 1983 de-nerving was banned in Switzerland but, Ted believes,

The operation was the greatest thing that ever happened to Wallaby four years ago when he became so lame that he was paralysed. Since he was de-nerved, he has never looked back, winning several Grand Prix and Puissances. If he had not been de-nerved, he would have been a total write-off.

Ted elaborates,

Some member of the FEI who has never owned or ridden a show-jumper in his life, sits on a committee and is ready to pass judgement. In a way it's like running a football team; it is all too easy to criticise what's going wrong, but just try running the team and keeping all the players together.

It is certain that Boomerang would not have won even one Hickstead Derby if he had not been de-nerved. On the way home from competing in Geneva, where Boomerang had been lame, Ted called at the home of wealthy show-jumping owner Leon Melchior and sold him. When Ted arrived home, Boomerang was crippled after the journey, which motivated Ted to ring Melchior. Ted said that Boomerang was so lame he didn't think Melchior ought to have him. But Melchior simply replied, 'Send him.' So Ted despatched Boomerang to Melchior who immediately had him de-nerved. After this Boomerang had five to six years of top international competition, winning all over Europe and the United States.

At the time, in the mid-seventies, de-nerving show-jumpers was newer and less common than it is today. If Ted and Liz had Boomerang now, and also Nick to ride him, because he needed a strong jockey, Liz says,

We would definitely have kept him and had him de-nerved ourselves with the knowledge we now have. Now if we had a high-calibre horse, at the first sign of him going lame, I would have him de-nerved. The point is that the earlier the operation is carried out the better, and also the lower down the better because the problem is slowed down. Ideally, the operation is carried out just above the coronet band at the side of the pastern. I wouldn't like to have to ride a horse that was de-nerved higher. The trotting horses in the States are sometimes de-nerved above the fetlock, but I wouldn't wish to jump such a horse because if it had lost the feeling in its fetlock, I don't think it would be very safe to jump.

Liz on Boomerang, seven years old, at his first international horse show at
Geneva, 1973, showing how fences should be cleared and, simultaneously, helping
Liz win the accolade of the show's leading lady rider. (*Findlay Davidson*)

Ironically, in view of the de-nerving ban that was operative in Switzerland in 1983, the man who made de-nerving fashionable was the Swiss veterinary surgeon Dr Stihl. He travelled all over Europe successfully de-nerving horses. But, in England, the operation has been carried out, even if on a relatively minor scale, for some time. One of Ted and Liz's vets, Geoffrey Brain, who has de-nerved several horses for them, told them that his father was occasionally given a broken-down horse which he would then de-nerve and have a fine hunter for nothing.

Liz does not think that the current permitted dosage level of bute is high enough. The official ruling is that a horse may not have more than four microgrammes per millilitre of blood plasma. She says, 'This is so small that the International Riders' Club want to get it raised, and also to have some leeway or a warning level, so that if a horse was found to be approaching the permitted limit, the rider would be fined but not banned.'

Predictably, substitutes for bute, such as Finadine whose presence is not presently tested for, are being used in some countries. Bute masks pain in rather the same way as aspirin relieves a headache. Ted describes the effect of the current permitted level as 'like taking just one whisky for a bout of 'flu or like a bird trying to fly on one wing'.

In show-jumping, when drugs are criticised, Ted takes the following line:

> I may perhaps agree about quieteners and stimulators, but when we come to bute, and/or one or two other pain-killing drugs which do the same job, there's a load of rubbish talked. What do you do with a horse with a touch of navicular? Shoot him? Turn him out in the field? Many of the best horses I've known have been no good until they are nine or ten years old and every one of them has either had bute or a drug with a similar effect, or been de-nerved and then continued competing for at least five or six years. To keep the job straight I think it should be written into a horse's passport if it's been de-nerved or is on bute, or its equivalent, for the simple reason that amateurs can get caught if they buy a horse that has been on bute. When they ride it, it doesn't go nearly as well. Why? Because the professional knows his job inside out and an amateur can be landed with a horse he

admired that doesn't go a yard. It should all be above board and open, not done secretly.

It has to be remembered that every horse's absorption rate is different and, with increasingly high prize-money available (£1,344,173 in Britain alone in 1982), riders are likely to be tempted into trying to find ways round the rules.

Ted has strong views about the FEI with regard to de-nerving and the use of bute:

> It's a pity the FEI is not run like the BSJA. If you ask me, the FEI is out of touch with the use of bute. Ireland's Trevor Coyle was suspended for using bute after telling the gospel truth about how much he gave his horse. After that the FEI dope-tested his horse and he was put out of the sport for six months, which to my mind was wrong when he'd told the truth. It's all too easy now to take a person's living and way of existence away from them.
>
> I wouldn't be too surprised if the top European riders broke away from the FEI in the mid-1980s, rather like the tennis players, unless the FEI's general attitude changes.

At the World Championships in Dublin in June 1982, the official veterinary surgeons suspected that Ted had doped If Ever and the horse was tested several times with negative results. If a horse has been de-nerved by a top-class vet, the de-nerving can be very hard to detect unless the area where the operation was performed is shaved. This is why both Ted and Liz feel that if a horse has undergone this operation the fact should be registered on its passport in case it is ever sold.

The Swiss and German authorities are among the most stringent. The Germans are anti-bute, as are the Swiss, but maybe not so vehemently. Close observers may wonder why most German horses' tails are so hideously shaved at the top of the dock. The answer is that pulling is prohibited on the grounds of cruelty.

WEARING OUT HORSES AND THE EXPENSE OF COMPETING

That horses are wearing out much too fast is a problem which is not always fully comprehended. At the Horse of the Year Show, the horses are expected to jump more or less a Grand Prix every single night, except that of the Puissance, which puts unreasonable pressure on them. They have to be ultra-careful and it's very hard to keep them running at top level, night in night out for a week.

A rider can only jump three horses at this show. Ted suggests,

Different horses for different classes would be a solution, another horse for the fun competitions, which we can't now include. We are the only people who pay so much to compete and it's the best riders like Liz, Nick, Harvey Smith, David Broome and Malcolm Pyrah that the public come to see. Without them there would be a much smaller gate. I pay £40 a box a horse per week and I know it would mean more stabling. The special turns, like jousting, are paid to entertain, but the show-jumpers are not. If we weren't there, I doubt so many would pay so much to see the supporting attractions.

The special attractions can cost £10,000 to £20,000 along with administration expenses. Some riders still want appearance money, I don't. But I think that free stabling and hotel rooms wouldn't be out of the way. It cost us £1,820 to enter, stable the horses and stay at the hotel near to the Horse of the Year Show in 1982. That didn't include looking after the grooms, and feeding them, and the horses.

The major English shows do not provide sufficient opportunities for the leading riders to give their best young horses experience. The Germans can take their youngsters to Aachen, which is their premier show, and jump them regularly through the week, but a similar opportunity does not occur at the London shows.

Liz says,

As it happened, I decided not to go to Rome in May 1982, but if I had, I could have taken my novice Domino, who is Grade B, and jumped him all week, his expenses and journey being paid.

But, if I wanted to take him to our international at the White City in July for the smaller classes, I would not be allowed to do so.

Liz has no doubt that the reason show-jumpers are now wearing out so quickly is the riders' own fault. In the old days, especially before the development of the World Cup, the horses used to get a winter rest. Now that does not often happen, because if a rider has a decent horse he wants to jump at Olympia, just before Christmas, and probably at a spring qualifier too. As the horse can't be casually pulled out of the field for a show, but must be prepared, fittened and compete prior to a major contest, it virtually means jumping all the year round if a spring venue and Olympia are to be included. To have a rest of any sort, three months are necessary, consisting of six weeks for the horse to be out and let himself down, and six weeks to be thoroughly rested.

Liz believes that few international horses now have the benefit of such a break because with human nature being what it is and prize money being so high, the element of greed creeps in. The sponsored riders also face the problem that the Christmas Olympia Championships are televised and so the companies involved want their riders to compete there.

COURSES AND STRAIN ON HORSES

Ted thinks that courses in England have tended to improve now that the poles are lighter than they used to be; the German courses have also improved and do not use such big poles. He rates the Olympic Games one of the worst competitions for horses:

If you are a runner or a swimmer, you run or swim a mile or a set distance in practice and do the same at the Olympics. But for the horses it's an entirely different ball game. The fences are often considerably higher and wider or the distances wrong, too long or short. After the Olympics I've seen, I wouldn't want to take a nice horse to jump.

His views are given substance by the fact that there are hardly any clear rounds and many of the winners are seldom the same afterwards and never have quite the same enthusiasm to jump.

Ted adds,

> Nick jumped the guts out of Maybe at the Substitute Olympics in Rotterdam in 1980. He was one of the only three horses to have a double clear in the Prix des Nations but the FEI gave him little recognition for his achievement. That just has to be wrong.
>
> The strain on a horse at a meeting like the European Championships can be demanding too: two rounds in the Nations' Cup on the Friday and then maybe three in the Grand Prix on the Sunday for the individual title. Five rounds over big courses in three days is my idea of asking too much from any horse.

STABLING AT SHOWS

Beyond question, the greatest expense the riders now incur competing at British shows is the stabling; the prices have become extortionate, an absolute rip-off at figures around £12 per horse per night. Liz explains,

> The difficulty is that one firm has almost established a monopoly, so they can charge these shows what they like, and get it. Some of the better shows try and subsidise the riders a little bit but the situation has got rather out of hand.

For a big show-jumping équipe that requires six or eight stables at a show, this is an immense handicap. A £250 stabling fee for a show is not unusual. Usually, this has to be paid two months before the show takes place with no rebate if horses are unable to jump and the boxes unused.

Additionally, some of the stables are a disgrace with chewed-off bits and cracked planks that have not been repaired since the previous year. Mangers are rare but nails sticking out at odd, dangerous positions are not. Liz continues,

> Competition is always healthy and if there wasn't a monopoly they'd soon be cheaper and better serviced. One of the latest

John Whitaker walks down the centre aisle of the stables where the British horses were housed during the FEI Volvo World Cup Holland final in Vienna, 1983.
(*Liz Edgar*)

dodges at some shows is that when you arrive you are charged a supplementary fee for the straw bedding already in the boxes.

Even at the Royal International and Horse of the Year Shows, where the top riders are key figures in bringing in the crowds, the stabling fees mean that the leading British riders are subsidising the foreigners who get free stabling; but if the top British did not compete, there would be no show.

QUALIFYING FOR MAJOR BRITISH SHOWS

Another concern is that British riders are limited on the horses they can take to the Royal International. If they have two top horses and a good Grade B horse the latter cannot go to the Royal International because there is a rule which does not permit this, yet invited foreigners get preferential treatment as they can jump any grade of horse.

'An international rider is not going to take a young horse to a show like the Royal International if it isn't sufficiently able for the lesser classes. If it were permitted, it would be one way of giving a promising young horse experience,' Liz spells out. Before this rule came along Liz jumped Boomerang at the Royal International when he was a Grade B horse and he was in the money. Now such a horse would be barred entry but what better experience could a nice youngster have?

Now a horse must have won so much money or be of a certain grade before he can compete at major shows. To compete at Olympia in 1982 a horse had to have won £1,000 that year; to compete at Birmingham in 1983, to have been Grade A on 1st January 1983.

While £1,000 is not a high figure for a made horse that is jumping regularly, if a rider has a youngster he thinks might make an international, he does not want to be chasing money and forever bashing round against the clock in the formative years of the horse's career.

At Birmingham in April 1983, Lesley could not ride her third horse Flame, by the same sire as Frederic Cottier's Flambeau and who was quite capable, because he was at the top of Grade B but not quite Grade A, although he was jumping really well. This meant that Wallaby's rest had to be cut short and he was brought in from the field to provide Lesley with a third horse.

Liz explains her views:

Although Wallaby proved magnificent in the Puissance carrying Lesley over 7 feet 1 inch to victory over Harvey Smith on Sanyo Technology, this was hardly the point; it would have been much more helpful if Flame had been able to jump in the minor third classes. This rule was made to prevent a few riders abusing the privilege of having a little freedom, but does mean that owners who would only enter their horses in classes commensurate with their horses' ability suffer for the others. One idea for the future could be an adjudicating committee to decide which horses could go. The problem here is that no member would want to say a horse could not compete, whereas the organisers can hide behind a rule and no one is blamed.

Grade B horses, those who should be encouraged, are almost a lost grade. Educated riders would never enter a Grade B at a show like Birmingham unless it was up to the task because they would not want to make a fool of themselves in public. Liz illustrates the point:

> If international riders have two horses correctly qualified for the three major British indoor shows, they should be allowed to bring a third horse, even if he's a novice, provided they think he's up to the questions that will be asked in the third classes. Riders won't pay over £40 for the stabling at such a show if they don't think their horse is worth it.

THE BRITISH TEAM MANAGER, RONNIE MASSARELLA

Ever since Forever had sufficient experience, Liz has been a frequent British team rider and so knows team manager Ronnie Massarella well. One of the reasons that Massarella, the kind, but firm Yorkshireman of Italian ancestry, has enjoyed such a long run as senior team manager is because he has the knack of welding even the most obtuse or divergent four riders into a squad who strive desperately to help each other and win team contests for Britain.

SELECTION

Liz thinks that in the early eighties, selection was the most open. The Selection Committee in 1983 was General Sir Cecil Blacker, John Blakeway, David Broome, Douglas Bunn, Graham Fletcher, Ronnie Massarella, Malcolm Pyrah, Peter Robeson, Miss J.B. Taylor, and Col. Guy Wathen.

Liz believes that,

> There should be at least one rider on the Selection Committee and you could not have a better choice than my brother, David Broome, or Malcolm Pyrah, who know which horses can jump, and will not purposely send the wrong horse to the wrong place. They don't mind telling you what they think or why a decision was taken, especially Malcolm, he doesn't ever mince his words.

That's good because you know exactly where you are.

At the beginning of each season the riders are asked which international shows they would like to visit and put their names down for them on forms which are then returned to the Selection Committee. In January 1983, when team manager Ronnie Massarella talked to the six riders he thought his four for European Championships would come from, he indicated the major venues where he hoped they would compete. This was for two reasons: because the courses would be suitable for the championship build-up; and also to have the riders competing together to engender the all-important team spirit.

'The hardest team for selection is probably Calgary,' says Liz. 'The journey to Canada is really the cream of the outdoor season, so everyone wants to go there, but if you are going well enough you will usually make it.'

Ted concurs with Liz that there are few if any problems with the present selection system. Whereas years ago it was very difficult, especially for the younger riders, to get anywhere, now everyone gets a chance to jump abroad.

THE BSJA

The present regime at the British Show Jumping Association comes in for praise by Liz and Ted. Liz clarified her reasons,

> Everything is so open and straight; it has never been better. All the members from the internationals down to weekend competitors are looked after to the best of the Association's ability. And there's no favouritism: I've been fined £2 for not registering a horse before he's jumped, just like 'Little Charlie' down the road.

Ted agrees but volunteers,

> There are seldom any radical changes in England. The Rules Committee has a meeting and it's agreed that certain changes should be recommended. But often, six months later, no changes have been made. So why bother? Overall I think the BSJA have

worked out everything so it's ninety-nine per cent right but sometimes changes are for the good.

The worst thing that happened recently was George Hobbs' death in 1981, because as a former international who made many of his own horses, he understood the riders' reasoning and backed us up at committee meetings.

THE FEI

In common with many of the leading riders, Ted has little enthusiasm for the FEI, the international governing body of the horse world whose base is in Berne, Switzerland. He feels that one problem is that a number of FEI officials do not have sufficiently close understanding of the problems riders encounter. Liz illustrates the problem:

> At the World Cup final in Vienna in 1983, the conditions in the arena were rock-hard, with stones in the sand. The riders asked for shavings to be added and these were promised, but when they jumped on the first night, nothing had been done. The next day, Ted, at the request of the riders, met an official at the entrance to the ring to try and get conditions improved. The official said he'd been riding in the park that morning and was an experienced horseman. 'Yes,' said Ted, 'but I'll bet you didn't ride on the cobblestones.'
>
> Also, the stables, which were some of the worst I've ever seen, were really dangerous for the horses, especially as there were stallions among them.

There was a new FEI rule out in 1983 which, like many riders, Ted abhorred and considered typical of the FEI. Briefly, in certain competitions where there are two fences separated by a difficult related distance, after the horse jumps the first fence, if it misses its stride it may circle and come back into the second fence unpenalised except for possible excess time faults. 'I've no doubt that in a minute, the FEI will realise what they have done and amend the rule, but it just isn't good enough,' Ted commented.

Another grouse Ted has is vets having the authority to take major decisions when 'they have never experienced running a show-jumping stable'.

THE INTERNATIONAL RIDERS' CLUB

Like most of the show-jumpers, Liz thinks that the International Riders' Club, which was founded in 1977, is basically a good idea although it has not yet gathered up sufficient strength. In 1983, the Honorary President was David Broome and Vice-president, Paul Schockemohle. The International Riders' Club's achievements include the continuing use of bute. Without their support there is little doubt that it would have been banned in 1980 or 1981.

Lister Welch, who manages the Club, was an ideal choice. His wide background includes stage direction at Glyndebourne, running his own agency and representing sports personalities, such as Naomi James, and from 1970 onwards, David Broome. It was the latter who asked if he would become Managing Director of the International Riders' Club.

The former World Champion's choice could not have been better for Lister Welch has the interests of show-jumping very much at heart and offers a welcome strength of purpose and wealth of innovatory ideas not always evident among the sport's entrepreneurs.

One example of the Club's growing authority came at the World Championships at Dublin, in 1982, when the immediate requests of David Broome and Paul Schockemohle concerning inadequate practice facilities resulted in an improved area being provided.

'As long as the Club doesn't suggest any strikes or Communist-type activity,' Liz is behind them, but she would not support any such withdrawal going back to her belief that, 'in the show-jumping job, you are on your own and that's the best way to be: you take your own decisions'.

At the Paris Indoor Show in December 1982, the riders went on strike one afternoon because they considered the going unsuitable. Liz competed at the same show in 1981 when the going was also dreadful:

On the first day in the jump-off I turned Forever to a parallel and the ground was so bad he fell straight through it, so I didn't jump him on the second or third days. End of saga. I simply said that the ground wasn't good enough for me to compete, but I did not want to start a strike. Whenever I walk a course and find it too big, I make up my own mind and say, 'Not today, thank you.' I don't make a fuss; I don't try and get the course made smaller; I do my own thing. It's the same with my novices, if I arrive at a show and the ground's wrong, I don't say anything, I just don't jump. I might explain why if an official asks, but I don't try to make anyone agree with me.

FINDING NEW HORSES

Finding new horses and making them is an art at which the Everest Stud has been outstandingly successful, especially where young horses are concerned. But finding horses in the eighties is not nearly as easy as it was a decade or two ago. Liz recalls,

> Then, at a small county show you might see a girl riding a horse that wasn't going quite right for her. It would have had some experience and more often than not, you could buy it for a reasonable figure. Then, if a decent jockey such as Ted or David got on, it wouldn't get the better of them and you had an immediate winner.

Today such a purchase is almost impossible because this type of horse does not seem to be about, and if a rider finds one, the horse's owner is far more likely to hang on, harbouring hopes of an astronomical figure. The Everest Stud's last purchase of this type was If Ever in June 1980. He was a difficult horse and won classes for the boy who rode him but was inconsistent until Nick had the ride.

Ted now faces an additional problem because as soon as the owner of a horse he is interested in buying realises the identity of the would-be purchaser, the price is prone to double, the seller thinking that if Ted is after the horse, it must be good and so he decides to keep it.

CHAPTER NINE

COMPETING ABROAD – ANTWERP, 1983

The syndrome illustrated in the movie, *If it's Tuesday, it must be Belgium* – a story about a group of American tourists 'doing' Europe, rapid style, another day, another country – could well be applied to show-jumpers, but more on a weekly basis. The weekly international schedule in March 1983 was: Week 1, s'Hertogenbosch, Holland; Week 2, Antwerp, Belgium; Week 3, Dortmund, Germany; Week 4, Geneva, Switzerland; 31st March, opening of Birmingham, England.

Liz and Lesley had received invitations to compete in Belgium, from Armand Tyteca, the Antwerp Show director. The invitations were readily accepted. There was to be a World Cup Qualifier, and Liz was keen to jump Forever who had only been in work five weeks since his first proper winter rest for four years. This would sharpen him up for Birmingham three weeks later. Moreover, it would be Lesley's first, full senior international show on the Continent.

So at 5.30 a.m. on Tuesday, 8th March the Antwerp party, including myself, sets out from Leek Wootton in a Mercedes horse-box with five horses loaded up. The horses are Forever; Lesley's then mounts-FMS Barbarella, Whato and Killarney Boy; and Caramelle, who has been sold into Belgium and is to be collected by his new owner when we arrive at the showground. The £40,000 floating horse palace is lit up as we glide down the drive from Rio Grande into the swirling fog.

Soon we arrive in Coventry and, as we hit the M45, which is the M1 link, the fog balloons against the lorry under the amber-coloured glow of the street lights.

The box had been loaded up the previous day by Lesley and Lisa, Liz's groom, who always travels with her. All the horses' requirements were included – bridles hanging on the wall; brushes,

medicaments, etc. in a giant trunk labelled, 'There are only two
things wrong with a man, everything he does and everything he
says.' All our cases are up in the Luton, the area over the cab, out
of the way.

The horses' hard food is stored in cupboards outside, as is their
hay supply for the show. The shows do provide hay, and although
it turned out to be sweet and first class at Antwerp, most riders
prefer to use their own whenever possible, so the horses' diet
remains unchanged. On the roof are tightly packed bags of wood
chips for their bedding.

'All the horses were fed at 4.45 a.m. and I told the girls to give
them a bellyful of hay last night,' says Liz. They are not fed while
travelling, only when the box is still.

Liz handles the monster lorry and its eight gears with an enviable
authority that would be lauded by any trans-European lorry
driver. 'It's just like·a Mini but easier to drive,' she says denigrat-
ingly, 'so light, with the power steering.' We are soon on the M1
progressing smartly down the middle lane, passing a series of
slower lorries on the inside. 'I doubt anything will pass us,' Liz
assesses correctly.

Keeping awake on long journeys is sometimes a problem. A
sizeable collection of cassettes is one answer, and so are constant
cups of tea and coffee. Both Liz and Ted are fervent Country and
Western fans and soon Lesley and Lisa are backing Glen Campbell
as he swings into 'Rhinestone Cowboy'.

The layout of the inside of the front of the box is more comfortable than one would expect. At a pinch, two can sit on the passenger seat in front. You can walk between the driving seats to the
living area behind, which is a small comfortable room.

The living area contains a sink surrounded by cupboards above,
below, and at the sides, and many drawers. Just like any kitchen,
it contains china, glasses, cutlery, cleaning materials and food. In
the corner there is a fridge and, by the sliding door that separates
the area from the horses, a fair-sized mirror which is used largely
for checking hat, jacket and tie when changing to go and compete.
One side of the area has a comfortable bench seat that can accommodate four. There is storage space underneath and cupboards for
clothes above. Another two people can sit in the area behind the
driving seats and there is also a stool. A table is kept stored away

and opens up when fitted onto an aluminium pole that slots into a recess in the floor.

It is Lesley's job to keep this area clean by brushing the carpets and seats and seeing that the food supply is renewed after each show. And, perhaps even more importantly, that the rolls of Polo mints that are kept in a drawer for the horses are replenished.

Dawn breaks as we near London, revealing fields dazzlingly white with a hard frost, but the heater is effective, and we are warm and comfortable.

We go straight through London, down Park Lane, round Hyde Park Corner leaving Buckingham Palace on our left before crossing the Thames over Vauxhall Bridge. We are quickly out at Greenwich Common as the rush-hour traffic crawls by in the right-hand lane.

Four hours after leaving Rio Grande, at 9.30 a.m. we arrive at Dover with plenty of time in hand to check in and catch the 12.30 p.m. Dover–Zeebrugge Townsend Thoresen boat.

Processing the horses' papers at the Customs can, and often does, take forever. In the past British show-jumpers have been delayed for as long as forty-eight hours at the French–Spanish border; this is one reason there is seldom a rush to make the long wearisome trip to Spain.

The first move is to check in with the police at their office. They ask how many horses we have and make sure we have the necessary health certificates and passports. All the show-jumpers' travel arrangements are usually made by Gordon Ashman of Pedens, the Newbury based firm of horse transporters.

For crossings from Dover to the Continent, Pedens work in conjunction with Lep Travel who are their official agents at the Dover docks. Lep's Silvie Scott soon came to see us through the formalities. The horses' passports contain detailed descriptions, both written and drawn, for identification. The health certificates will be vital for the authorities at Antwerp, and it is essential that the horses have been inoculated against Coggins disease – equine infectious anaemia – the presence of which is shown by blood tests.

The organisation is efficient and half an hour later we are parked near the yellow-funnelled boat by a large double-layered lorry and an accompanying trailer-load of sheep. An official explains that all

Liz's groom Lisa and Lesley mixing a feed for the horses on the dock side at Dover as the box waits to be loaded onto the Zeebrugge boat. (*Ann Martin*)

The horsebox parked in the boat on the way to Antwerp. (*Liz Edgar*)

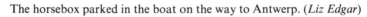

the animals will be put on last because workmen have been welding and burning off paint in the boat and the smell will be rather obnoxious until the boat sails.

Lisa decides that this is the ideal moment to feed the horses. Out onto the tarmac come nuts, bran, chaff and sugar beet, pre-soaked in a metal container. The feed is mixed and given in hook-on portable mangers.

The horses have only just finished their food when the signal is given to drive aboard. Followed by the sheep, we proceed down the ramp and park on the left-hand side of a group of huge Hungarian juggernaut lorries that are on their way home to Budapest.

Lisa puts down the ramp to give the horses plenty of air. A helpful officer comes up and tells her she can fetch water for the horses from the nearby crew area to save a long walk. The horses enjoy their first drink in eight hours. Forever plunges his face in up to his noseband and emerges happily dripping water all over. The pale sun has made the air close in the box, so the horses' top rugs are turned back at the corners. We leave the horses in the box and go up to the first deck, heading for the restaurant.

Including a leisurely lunch, the four hours pass quite quickly. The girls return to check the horses at least every half hour. The sea is as calm as a mill pond. We return to the box to find the horses completely relaxed and contentedly dozing in the half light of the lower deck.

The driver in charge of the sheep chats to us, probably because we are the only other people travelling animals. Sadly his are destined for the pot. 'Why couldn't they be killed at home and the meat transported on the hook rather than the hoof?' Liz enquires with concern. She receives the unsatisfactory answer that they make their wretched journey because of EEC regulations.

We are soon off the boat at Zeebrugge and parked alongside the baleful-eyed sheep by the Customs House. A well-informed Belgian has been detailed to speed us on our way and it takes only a quarter of an hour for the horses to proceed through Customs.

The port officials come in to inspect the horses but a cursory glance is all they need, coming up the steps at the side of the box into the area in front of the horses. Forever always stands at the front of this section and the horses are divided by movable head

portions of leather on a solid frame. After the first two horses there
is a division the width of the box, which will prevent them from
falling on each other should the brakes have to be applied suddenly. The horses are well accustomed to travel so there is scant
risk of kicking. They know both the routine and their companions
very well and take journeys in their stride. Forever makes the most
of the forward position looking as beguiling as possible in the hope
of a Polo mint.

At 5.15 p.m. Lisa puts down the corners of the horse rugs as it
is getting decidedly chilly. Dusk quickly falls as we drive north out
of Zeebrugge through an area of flat dykeland dotted with huge
gaunt châteaux, to the motorway.

One and a half hours later we are in Antwerp, Belgium's biggest
port, sited inland up the River Amstel. A city of over 600,000
inhabitants, it is a mass of flashing lights and tinselled motorway
intersections. We approach on the E3 and change to the E10.

'Pass under a tunnel,' Nick had instructed Liz on the phone
from Antwerp. 'Soon afterwards you will see the Sports Palace
straight ahead shortly after passing the Holiday Inn on the right.'
He had arrived earlier from competing at s'Hertogenbosch together with John Whitaker. In the dark we do not notice the tunnel
and it takes much longer than we expect before the dimly-lit, huge,
green conical dome of the big building, which is totally unsigned,
looms out of the darkness on our left.

Leaving the motorway, Liz executes a neat 'U' turn between
sturdy trams and speedy traffic to arrive at the main entrance of
the Sports Palace, which is closed with no one there to direct us.
Liz drives round the back where we can see marquees which must
house the stables. Turning into the complex down a narrow lane,
we find ourselves by a sizeable river basin packed with boats. The
boxes lay immediately ahead of us but our route is halted by a
stout row of concrete bollards.

Two figures loom out of the dark and thankfully we recognise
them as the girl grooms of Eddie Macken and Paul Darragh. They
tell us to turn round and look for a muddy lane that is the entrance
to the stables.

Undaunted, Liz turns the giant box on a sixpence in what we
later learn is a car-driving practice area, after yet another 'U' turn
we retrace our tracks looking for the entrance we must have passed.

A dirty, insignificant gap in the railings seems the likely answer and following a dashing third 'U' turn across a busy intersection, we are at last approaching the stables, parallel with the overhead E10 motorway.

As we come close, the more than welcome sight of Nick emerges from the shadows. Liz slips over into the centre front seat as Nick jumps up and drives the box into the unloading area some twenty yards from the horses' boxes.

Caramelle, who comes down the ramp first, is led straight off to other stables to be collected by his new owners. We do not see him again. We lead the remaining four horses down from the box, then through a very narrow entrance flap which worries them not a jot, into one of the big blue-and-white striped marquees.

Susie, Nick's groom, appears and gives a hand; Nick's horses are further down on the other side of the main alley. Forever decides he needs a roll, spending some time weighing up where to get up and down safely in his small but solid temporary box. We all watch as he carefully lowers himself in his selected spot, then gets up and shakes himself free of a cloud of wood chips.

The horses' rugs are straightened, the horses are fed and watered and their bandages checked. Nick moves the horse-box into a place he has reserved, next to his own under the motorway. Although the traffic is lessening, there is a steady clonking as cars and lorries pass along over a section where there are gaps left in the foundation girders for expansion.

Lesley and Lisa will be sleeping in the box throughout the show so perhaps it is fortunate they were up at 4 a.m. and will be so tired that they will not hear the noise. Nick, who is a fiend for cleanliness, sweeps out the horses' area of the box and also brushes the part where we travelled. His particular friend on the circuit is John Whitaker, and as usual when abroad, they are travelling together in one of the Everest boxes. Malcolm Pyrah appears and they all help Liz and me with our luggage, along a lengthy walk to the Sports Palace, straight through the arena, and up some steps to a café at the front of the building where we order a taxi.

The drive to the hotel takes twenty minutes. We check into our rooms at 10 p.m., sixteen and a half hours after leaving Leek Wootton, then go down to dinner in the restaurant with Malcolm, Nick and John. They tell us all about s'Hertogenbosch the previous week and a hilarious visit they made the preceding night to a chic Antwerp health club with show-jumper Ferdy Tyteca, son of the Show Director, Armand.

The plan on the first day is breakfast at 9.45 a.m. then out to the show. The Volvo cars that are meant to be laid on for transport to and from the show are not in evidence so we go in taxis. At £5 a trip, it will be too expensive to come back to the hotel during the day. It is a damp, cold, foggy, gloomy morning. We walk straight through the arena with David Broome and meet course designer Blair Williams who has come out to build for the European Young Riders' Classes.

Robert Puskas, architect designate of the World Cup final in Vienna the following month, is building for the Seniors, so the riders are keen to experience his type of track. The jumps look big. Blair says

Nick giving Radius a breath of fresh air by the River Amstel during the 1983 Antwerp Horse Show. (*Ann Martin*)

the one we are standing by is the only junior one. 'Maybe,' quips Malcolm Pyrah, 'but it's the only one that looks jumpable to me.'

Approaching the boxes, we meet Lisa. She sounds really cheerful but looks a trifle jaded after a fitful sleep under the motorway and says, 'It sounded as though giants were kicking round oil drums all night.'

The first move is to check in at the Secretariat, collect the passes – plastic wrist bands that give the wearer free access to stables, collecting ring, the funnel, riders' stand and various stadium facilities. There are also invitations to a special riders' lunch in the chic Maison Van der Boeur, and meal tickets which could be used at the restaurants in the adjacent hall of stands and shops or the small café–restaurant at the entrance. The grooms also have passes and meal tickets.

Liz's right knee has become loose jointed after an accident incurred a long time ago with Uncle Max. As a result she must always be careful not to land on it awkwardly or jump down from a height. Three weeks beforehand the young Domino ducked out in the middle of a double in a competition and the sudden swerve put her knee out although Liz remained firmly in situ. A high-powered course of physiotherapy and massage got her back into the saddle in time for Antwerp, but the knee still needs regular treatment from the ultra-sonic machine that is part of Liz's luggage wherever she travels to compete.

When she got up that morning, Liz treated her knee, and now, before putting on her chaps to work Forever, she redoes her bandage to be sure it is tight enough to give support.

Lisa is just finishing grooming Forever as Liz arrives at his stable. He always bites and kicks when brushed but is otherwise perfect in the stable, gentle as a kitten. As Lisa saddles him up and puts on his protective boots, Liz dangles a shiny green apple she brought for him from the hotel breakfast table and Forever produces his usual beguiling look.

As he is led out by Lisa into the fresh air he spooks as a 'Queen Mary' of cars clanks along the overhead motorway. The waste ground where the boxes and stables are sited is a complete shambles, covered with cast-out rubbish; the Irish grooms are, as ever, lungeing their charges in the middle of the jumble.

Lisa legs Liz up into the saddle and she goes straight into the marquee-covered schooling area where John Whitaker on Clonee Temple, Malcolm Pyrah on Diamond Seeker, Eddie Macken on Carroll's Royal Lion and a large long-haired blonde groom with thick thighs on a heavy chestnut are among those schooling their horses.

Forever seldom needs much work and with a five-day show in prospect, Liz plans to compete with him three times: that night, which is Wednesday, Friday and then in the big one, the Antwerp Grand Prix which is combined with an FEI Volvo World Cup Holland Qualifier on Sunday afternoon.

After working out their horses, all the British riders and Australian Kevin Bacon have lunch together in the friendly café at the entrance. David muses on the problems of hanging around all day long at indoor shows where so much of the jumping is at night:

Relaxing in the lorry between classes. (*Bob Langrish*)

'You keep eating and having cups of tea and coffee to kill time. You have too much, put on weight and tend to get very bored being on an isolated showground from 9 a.m. until midnight.'

After lunch the riders gather in Liz's box and, following a cup of tea, disperse to get ready for the opening class. Success in an early class always lifts a country's morale and Nick set the ball rolling by winning the opening Audi-Porsche Speed Class on Jet Lag, the first of the seven classes the British were to claim from the total of eleven.

The following Bank Brussel Lambert jump-off class was Forever's first 1983 competition. Liz was delighted when unhurried, he jumped flawlessly to finish second to Ferdi Tyteca on Ransome.

By 11.15 p.m. the riders have changed and are back in the entrance café ready for food. On the television a blue movie from Berlin is being shown, all feet and knees and too many hands. The waitress asks us to move to the table area reserved for late diners and the conversation turns to home. Most of the riders telephone home every day from Continental shows, certainly Liz and Nick do and Nick has just called his wife Sarah to tell her of Jet Lag's success. John talks of his new baby son Robert John who was born in January 1983, and describes how his house is set high on the Yorkshire Moors at Upper Cumberworth, 1,200 feet above sea-level. Suddenly Liz realises that the declarations which must be made the night before a competition have not been done and Nick willingly runs back to the Secretariat before it closes to ensure they are lodged in time. We get back to the hotel at 2 a.m.

Thursday proves a day of much hanging around the show-ground. The first class is scheduled for 7.15 p.m., the second at 9.45 p.m. After exercising the horses it's back to the café for a long lunch with Eddie Macken and Paul Darragh. The meal ends at 4.15 p.m. Afterwards, David who has discovered the generator on his box is not working properly, disappears rather disconsolately to tackle the problem, which is not easy on desolate waste land.

Several of this tight little band of riders who travel to shows together have their own nick-names. David is 'Basil', John 'Spot', Malcolm 'Hitler' and practically everyone calls Lesley 'Tulip'.

Nick is a card fanatic and soon he, Spot, Hitler, Liz and myself are engrossed in a game of 'Cheat', which involves trying to see everyone else's hands as well as guessing who is cheating. The cards are a beautiful red pack engraved 'Malcolm Pyrah' in gold. 'Keep your greasy fingers off my cards,' warns Malcolm as Liz cuts her favourite Christmas cake and cheese to eat with a cup of tea.

Looking out of the front window of the box provides varied entertainment as the last competitors arrive. Gunther, West German Olympic medallist Fritz Ligges' groom, puts down a very steep ramp at the side of Fritz's horse-box and guides down his horses' huge heavy trunk of accoutrements which is on wheels, by means of a small remote-control electronic machine held in one hand.

Then a model of the largest, most powerful Mercedes saloon car glides by, pulls up and out steps diminutive Austrian Hugo Simon, dwarfed by his gleaming black monster of a car. 'Now we really have seen everything,' says Nick.

Harvey Smith flies in from Yorkshire just in time to walk the course and win the Accumulator on the acrobatic Sanyo Shining Example, who executes his circus bow on receiving his rosette. In the following competition, John Whitaker makes it a British double, winning the Dunhill Cup on the mare Clonee Temple. Later the alternatives are dining in the hotel or a visit to the Cartier Discothèque.

The Volvo transport is now in evidence but the cars are quickly taken. Harvey and Kevin Bacon sail off in state in a half-empty estate car leaving David, Liz and I stranded, the only alternative being to walk to the entrance café and order a taxi. 'That's the way it goes abroad,' says Liz, 'every rider for himself.'

On Friday morning in the hotel lobby we meet a moustachioed Volvo driver called Francis who helps us considerably over the next three days. His pidgin English is a welcome relief after the local Flemish language. He is justly proud of Antwerp and waves at a tall building, saying, 'You see that. It's Belgium's biggest skyscratcher.'

After a sumptuous riders' lunch where Liz is given a handsome umbrella and useful tote bag, the pace starts to hot up with the arrival of Ted. He flew out of England early that morning, since when he has driven several hundreds of miles up and down the Belgian motorways with François Mathy in search of new horses.

Not long before the jumping starts, David and Jane Kingsley, who seldom come to foreign competitions, fly in; they are especially friendly with Armand Tyteca whose business interest is the shipping insurance company he founded in 1953. The final arrivals are Cliff Cox and his wife, owners of FMS Barbarella, the mare Lesley will ride in the Grand Prix.

They picked the right night as the main competition, the ITT Prize, results in a British one, two, three, headed by Liz on Forever, with Malcolm on Towerlands Anglezarke separating the Everest horses, as Nick was third with Radius. After Forever nearly fell over the first jump, away from the collecting ring, he never put a foot wrong, but Malcolm thought he had been fast enough to win. Ted is most pleased with Radius's performance;

after a year off in 1982 being fired, Ted's 1983 orders are to take him relatively steadily, because, all being well, he sees him as a 1984 Grand Prix prospect.

For the celebration party there could be no better venue than Maison Van der Boeur, which must be the most élite of the restaurants on the world's show-jumping circuit. Malcolm Pyrah and John Whitaker join the Everest group of the Kingsleys, Ted, Liz and Nick for a meal so superb that it becomes the riders' custom to eat there the remaining two nights of the show.

A combination of fine food and wine, coupled with success-spiced fatigue, make for an entertaining evening which lasts until we are the last occupied table at 3.30 a.m., an hour at which both Volvo cars and taxis are not unreasonably conspicuous by their absence.

The Mâitre D counsels us not to worry, all will be resolved. As we hover around the entrance, the jokes continue. Just after 4 a.m. our transport arrives. We walk out into the chill early morning air to find a specially chartered bus at our command. Piling in with a degree of relief we are safely back in our hotel rooms half an hour later. An incredible ending to a perfect day.

Saturday is inevitably the calm before the major contest, the Grand Prix. Forever, called 'Ginge' by Everest inmates, is given a rest and only led out morning and afternoon by groom Lisa, who is enjoying her first show abroad with Liz.

The evening ends in glory for Lesley McNaught when riding the Countess of Inchcape's Whato. She shares first place with Switzerland's Walter Gabathuler on Beethoven in the Moet et Chandon Puissance, both narrowly failing to clear 2.20 metres, approximately 7 feet 2 inches. A crowd of 10,000 saw her struggle valiantly back into the saddle when Whato jerked her onto his offside on landing.

At a lighthearted dinner in Maison Van der Boeur that night with Harvey and David completing the group, a bargain is struck that if an English rider wins the Grand Prix which combines the World Cup Qualifier, he or she will stand dinner for all the British contingent at Maison Van der Boeur on the final night.

Afterwards Ted and Liz have a nightcap in the Crest Hotel and chat to Austrians Thomas Fruhmann and Hugo Simon, and Kevin Bacon who are at adjacent tables. 'Just a minute,' interrupts

Ted in the middle of a story Cliff Cox is telling, 'I must get some chips.' It doesn't take long to take a handful from the plate of Holland's Robert Ehrens who is eating nearby with his compatriot Toni Ebben.

Sunday is the big day with the Grand Prix scheduled for 4.30 p.m. Belgian Edgar Cuepper, who won the s'Hertogenbosch equivalent on Cyrano the previous week, describes the television coverage of the Puissance to Lesley: 'I was at home and saw you hit the top and Whato screw up behind. I looked away and a little later looked again. To my surprise you were still on the saddle, what happened?'

David and Jane Kingsley join us for coffee in the horse-box and tension rises as the crucial competition approaches and the brightly striped plastic fence poles, piled like pikastiks on the arena skirt, gradually disappear into the ring.

A strong smell of fried onions from a nearby hamburger stall pervades throughout the funnel, riders' stand and surrounding seats. It is doing a roaring trade.

Malcolm, who won here last year, gives a repeat performance of three clears on Towerlands Anglezarke, beating Cuepper and Cyrano in the second jump-off by over a second. Forever, who was 'dead' because he was not yet one hundred per cent fit when Liz went to warm him up for the final round, was a creditable fifth in the fastest time, rather unluckily knocking a pole off the third fence.

Ted had followed his usual practice of giving If Ever a work-out on the preceding day, and the little roan, who is very light on his feet, was jumping like a cat with Nick carefully picking his stride to the degree that he misjudged the time, collecting a one-quarter time fault in the first jump-off.

The Kingsleys and Ted rush off as the class ends to drive to Brussels and catch the last plane home. The riders collect their prizes, which include a large ITT television set and two twenty-two carat gold miniatures of the rearing horse that is the emblem of the show – one has a diamond on a hoof.

Lesley and Lisa have to pack the box ready to leave in the morning and will eat in the cafeteria afterwards. In Maison Van der Boeur, Malcolm is more than pleased to host a victory dinner with Liz, Harvey, David, John and Nick as his guests.

Tomorrow everyone will go their separate ways: David flying

home to Wales; Harvey travelling on to Dortmund where the show opens three days later; Liz driving back to England; and John, Nick and Malcolm staying on one more day in Antwerp before travelling to Dortmund. 'Be sure they are keeping the stables up,' warns Harvey.

Once again the bus is summoned to take us back to the hotel in style. We are in bed at 12.30 a.m. ready to snatch three hours' sleep before the alarm goes all too soon at 3.30 a.m.

At 4 a.m. Liz and I meet Hickstead's Anita Arnett in the lobby. She is travelling in the box with us to Zeebrugge to catch the boat. Our taxi arrives on the dot and we are driven right up to the box as the last horse is being loaded.

At precisely 4.30 a.m., we drive off the filthy dirty waste land, leaving a large cloud of black dust in our wake, into totally deserted streets. Our only stop is on the motorway to top up with diesel; the tank holds forty gallons. The drive is totally in the dark. Lisa and Lesley make coffee all round and then fall asleep. It is 6.10 a.m. when we arrive at the docks. Our passports are checked, and then the horses' papers, by a roomful of jolly Belgians sipping coffee from Thermos flasks and listening to the radio.

As we drive on to the boat past cranes and muddy sand where seagulls are picking for worms in the beam of our headlights, there is the faint pale orange glow of dawn in the dark sky. When the box is parked, the ramp is lowered and the horses, who were fed at 3.30 a.m., are given a drink of water. The immediate need is sleep. Liz sets the duvet and pillows out and makes herself comfortable in the lorry while Lesley and Lisa go up to claim the two berths that are available for driver and co-driver of every lorry.

No one is ravenously hungry and we arrange to meet for breakfast at 10.00 a.m. for a meal that will also serve as lunch as the main object now is to get home as soon as possible. A full English breakfast is the order of the day. The dining room is empty and we eat our way through huge plates of eggs, bacon, sausages and tomatoes, toast and marmalade washed down with fruit juice, tea and coffee.

After a final visit to the duty-free shop for Liz to buy some more Bailey's Irish Cream while Lisa buys some chocolates for her mother, the familiar white cliffs come close so we go down to the box to wait for the boat to dock.

Shortly after 11 a.m. we drive cheerfully up the ramp, optimistically expecting to be back in Warwickshire by mid-afternoon.

Our passports are quickly checked, and Lisa who has the horses' passports and papers is directed to the equine clearance area. The customs men come in to search the box. 'I can't go in there, I'm afraid of horses,' shrieks a new recruit, but he does, his seniors behind him. They go through every cupboard in the box, casting a wary eye at Forever who mistakenly thought they might be good for at least one Polo mint.

We arrived at Dover at 10 a.m. English time. Three hours later at 1 p.m. we are still sitting in the wagon, like a great white whale stranded on a beach after a storm, as vast transporters from all over Europe and behind the Iron Curtain give full throttle and pass on towards their destinations through the pass-out barrier.

The horses were fed and watered soon after our arrival and now give the odd anxious scrape. Habitual travellers, and used to being on the move, they sense that something is amiss because they have been still for far too long. Such delays are undesirable for horses in transit as an irregular schedule renders them more susceptible to colic which can so easily turn into the usually fatal twisted gut.

The delay has arisen because travelling out, the box contained five horses, and now there are four. Forever, Barbarella and Whato are making the round trip, but Caramelle was already sold before leaving England and then the Irish cob Killarney Boy was sold in Antwerp. The fourth horse on the return trip is David Broome's Royale who is not going on with Mr Ross and Heatwave to Geneva.

The fact that his papers and passport are in order is to no avail. The officials, perhaps weary after seeing the Household Cavalry out to Germany in the morning, do not believe that Royale is Royale. Worse still, they do not or will not come and look at the chestnut and inspect him in relation to the official detailed marking plan in his passport which would confirm that he is Royale. Liz quite rightly decides we all need a restoring drink and we enjoy a cup of one of her special mixtures, coffee reinforced with Bailey's Irish Cream.

A horse to look out for in 1984, Nick and Radius executing a perfect bascule.

Just over four hours after we arrived at Dover, the horses are given the go-ahead after a delay which was both frustrating, unnecessary, tiring and time-consuming for all concerned. After all the hold-up, the London road is blocked. A diversion takes us to Folkestone which adds to our journey because it means we miss the motorway. The rush-hour is just getting underway as we hit London, so we go via Blackfriars Bridge rather than the direct central route, to avoid the traffic.

Fifteen hours after we left Antwerp we arrive home at Rio Grande in the dark in a torrential downpour. One of the advantages of the new building is that the box can be driven into the indoor school, the horses led out to their stables under cover, and all the contents of the box are kept dry as they are moved to the tack room.

Marie gives Forever a most welcome Polo mint and Liz's sister, Mary, who has driven up from Wales to collect Royale for David, puts him straight into her horsebox ready for the journey home to Mount Ballan.

In the kitchen there is a heartwarming domestic scene. The table is set, and Ted, who has been enjoying the last day's hunting of the season, is relaxing in the rocking chair having a drink. Julie is stirring a casserole on the Aga. Marie is seated at the table, sipping a glass of Californian rosé wine and sewing a waistcoat she is making, anxiously waiting for her mother to sit down. Yesterday was Mothering Sunday and on Liz's plate is a card addressed 'Mummy' with a present, some chocolates, underneath. Tired, but happy, Liz is home.

CHAPTER TEN

THE SHOW JUMPING YEAR

Although there is a very wide and ever-increasing choice of available shows at which to compete, Ted and Liz have, after trying most of them, become quite 'set in our ways' and go to almost the same ones every year.

January is by far the easiest month with a mixture of hunting and a few small local shows at the National Equestrian Centre, Stoneleigh, and Balsall Common, both of which are within five miles from home. Between these two there are shows most weekends and a few mid-week.

As the top horses are resting there is time to play around with, and educate the novices at these shows where there is probably only £10 if you win and no pressure. The Edgars take all the young horses and any of the others that they want to try, and Liz explains, 'Nick and I are more interested in seeing how the novices jump rather than winning at this stage.'

January running into February is the ideal time to take a holiday; Florida, and in 1983, Thailand, have been recent choices. Liz likes to relax in the sun.

During February work begins on the more experienced horses. The long business of quietly getting them fit is started by walking on the roads. They are all wormed and checked by the vet who comes and updates the horses' passports which have to be signed each year with details of their vaccinations or boosters. This is a vital procedure because without up-to-date documents, the horses cannot compete at international shows, even in England.

The February shows follow the same pattern as the January ones except that, hopefully, the youngsters are learning and going better and there is the chance to win the odd class without pushing the horses. This is a month that Liz cherishes for the all too rare opportunity to be at home with the growing sense of anticipation at the prospect of a new season.

She explains, 'All our hopes lie ahead. There are young and old horses jumping well; the older horses' coats start to gleam as they get fit and there are no disappointments – they come later on.'

March sees the beginning of the European circuit and final World Cup Qualifiers, but they largely concern Nick. For instance, in 1983 he was away for three weeks in March, travelling from s'Hertogenbosch to Antwerp then into Germany for Dortmund where the jumps are always formidable for so early in the season. He then missed the Geneva CSIO, coming home to be fully rested for the Birmingham International at Easter which was held the first weekend in April. Then he went on to the Swedish World Cup Qualifier at Gothenburg prior to the final in Vienna.

Nick opted out of Geneva because it might well have knocked the shine out of his horses for Birmingham the following week. Held at the National Exhibition Centre, Birmingham, is virtually a local show, being only twenty minutes' drive away and one at which sponsors Everest are keen he should give a good account of himself.

Liz managed to ride at Antwerp but concurred with Nick over Geneva for the same reason, although indoor shows such as Birmingham are not Forever's favourites. In March 1983, both Nick and Liz each had only one horse able to take on a really big track, namely If Ever and Forever.

The Birmingham International is Britain's first important fixture of the season and includes the spring British World Cup Qualifier. The horses stay at the show but Liz, Ted and Nick operate from home and drive over each day after working the horses which are not competing. It is a popular event with the show-jumpers because there are classes for all levels of horses, a comparatively rare phenomenon.

In 1982 the big liver chestnut Forecast gave his producers Ted and Liz considerable satisfaction by winning the Grade C Championship at Birmingham. He has since been sold and is progressing well for Derbyshire's Jane Mallaber.

Gothenburg always has to be considered carefully because of the twenty-four-hour sea journey. Liz says, 'If the sea blows up the horses are out sailing and have to suffer it.' Enduring bad travel conditions such as this can knock a horse's form for weeks.

The World Cup final at Vienna was Nick's first major 1983 target so the horses he took there did not jump outside beforehand to keep them used to the tighter distances of jumping indoors. This was not too big a problem as the first British outside international was the May Bank Holiday Hickstead.

The first outdoor show of any consequence for Liz is the Wales and West in mid-April. This has the added bonuses of a trip back home and a stay with her parents in their bungalow overlooking the permanent showground, which her father and brother founded in 1970. Predictably, when a show is run by a show-jumping family, there are opportunities for horses of all grades and excellent facilities, so the young horses travel down too.

Jon Doney is the senior course designer at the Wales and West and he excels at building the right courses for less-experienced horses. Liz might well take an international horse such as Forever to this early meeting if the money is enticing, or if, for instance, he needs a couple of rounds to get fit for Hickstead.

'My first big smack outside is Hickstead where we all get lined up for the Grand Prix,' Liz explains. The first two classes for the top horses at this meeting are normal classes warming up for the Grand Prix, but at Hickstead even these lesser ones usually carry £1,000 first prizes.

In 1982, the Hickstead Grand Prix ranged from £5,500 to £8,000 for the winner and Nick won all three on Everest If Ever which was no mean achievement. To compete there now Liz reckons that only one in-form, top-class horse is necessary because competitors are allowed to start only one in the Grand Prix.

Douglas Bunn has spent many thousands of pounds draining, levelling and landscaping the international arena and it rates among the world's best, a superb showpiece jumpable in almost all weather. As a former international, Bunn is well aware of the importance of scheduling classes for novices and always provides the right type of courses.

'But the same laudable conditions do not always prevail in the outer rings or collecting ring, which it has not yet been possible to develop to the same high standard for reasons of finance,' Liz continues. 'The going can sometimes turn out to be rough, wet, slippery or deep in the minor rings, but now that he has been appointed show manager, Dougie's son Edward will be trying to

At a meeting of the Wales and West Show, Ballan Lad, the pony who helped launch the Broome family to stardom with (from left to right) Millie (Mrs Broome), Fred Junior, David, Mary, Liz and Fred Senior (Mr Broome). In the background, Mount Ballan.

improve conditions.' However, the final decision of whether to compete or not does lie with the riders.

The next good show the stable attends is Newark and Nottinghamshire County Show. This is always held on the first Friday and Saturday in May on the often windswept former Winthorpe Airfield on the northern outskirts of Newark. There are some generously sponsored classes and it seldom clashes with any other big show.

In the second week of May comes Royal Windsor. Few of the jumpers like this venue, which is set on one of the most dramatic showgrounds in the country under the magnificent backcloth of

Windsor Castle. The problem for the show-jumpers in facing a five-day show is having to travel to it every day because there are no stables on the showground. The vast number of show exhibitors, such as those with hunters or Arabs, do not have that inconvenience because their classes are all on the same day for each category. The choices are staying with friends or at Ascot Racecourse, both of which mean bandaging and loading up the horses every day. Whether the lorry has to be driven for half an hour or two hours makes little difference, so the Everest horses now travel down daily because if they can't be on the showground, they are better at home. This means a daily four- to five-hour round trip which Ted is prepared to do because he is one of the few members of the jumping fraternity who like the show.

One advantage of competing from home is that the horses can be changed over and says Liz with obvious pleasure, 'We sometimes miss a day.'

This long-established show with its spectacular floodlit sessions which retain some of the elegance of the post-war era, has had difficulty attracting enough prize money to keep up with inflation and the other shows. But in 1983 there was a definite improvement with the final event, the Modern Alarms Classic, which Nick won on St James, carrying a first prize of £3,500.

One important competition here for Liz is the Ladies National Championship in which she has a fine record, but the competition simply has not moved with the times regarding prize money. In 1983 the first prize was £400, so Liz decided not to defend the title she won in 1982 with Forever. But the class the stable most enjoys winning is the Walwyn Novice Championship. One year, Ted took this class on Everest Jet Lag and was very proud to do so.

'The best thing about the following Devon County Show is the strawberries and the clotted cream,' Liz says pertinently, so it is now a very occasional rather than a regular visit. It is sited on the side of a hill where there is nowhere flat to ride the horses in and the going is often very muddy.

Towards the end of the month there may be a foreign show such as the Lucerne CSIO, and nearly always a visit to Stafford County Show where the courses generally suit the younger horses well.

The second Hickstead meeting of the year, which is held over the bank holiday weekend at the end of May, clashes on the

There are easier ways than walking. Nick at the Bath and West, 1982. (*Kit Houghton*)

Monday with the Surrey County Show at Guildford. Liz considers this one of the most pleasant one-day county shows: 'Firstly, because they love to have you; secondly, because they take all the care they can of the ground, providing the best conditions possible. It's always worth the drive.'

In early June comes the Royal Bath and West near Shepton Mallet. For Liz, 'This is the gem of all the outdoor shows. There's no doubt it's *the* outstanding county show. They don't take too many entries; they are very faithful to their old customers.' More than one have received a friendly reminding telephone call if they have not sent in their entries and the lists are nearly full.

'The whole set-up is perfect, the schedule runs to time and we are never rushed.' There are two classes a day, a major and a second one. The big class always carries attractive money and course designer Alan Oliver builds some good courses. Both young and speed horses are well suited to the jumps in the smaller classes, and 'the West Country people are some of the best. Even when they were totally flooded out, when there was all that rain and water everywhere, we didn't even pull out as we would do almost anywhere else; we stayed to give support and help them out.' Sadly, the super Chief Executive, Colonel James Myatt, died in February 1983. He brought this show up to its present top of the league position.

It's a shame that the lovely old well-established Suffolk County Show at Ipswich often clashes with the Bath and West. Unfortunately it's only a two-day show as opposed to a four-day show so it tends to lose out, but we always go if the dates are separate. I've been for years and years. My brother David and I used to travel to it from Wales together before Ted and I were married.

The South of England show is another event Liz rates highly and thoroughly enjoys. Reg Hughes, who runs the three-day show at Ardingly in Sussex, 'can't help us enough'.

As the show-jumpers progress round the country, those who live near the various showgrounds try and hold a party at home to entertain their show-jumping friends one night during their local show's run. Ray Howe, who used to ride for Douglas Bunn and now trains National Hunt horses, always entertains during Ardingly. He also invites the Edgars among others to a small barbecue at his house during most Hicksteads.

The mid-week Three Counties Show, which is held in the middle of June on the permanent ground under the shadow of the Malvern Hills is another show which Liz describes as 'a hassle' because it is one they travel to from home every day and doing the same trip across country rather than on a fast motorway, can get a bit boring. 'But,' she adds, 'Alan Oliver builds the courses so we can be sure they will be decent, but it's always very crowded even although they recently added another field to the box parking area.'

Below the ramparts of Cardiff Castle proud peacocks strut and scream, their privacy disturbed by the arrival of the show-jumpers for the Cardiff Show in June. Speaking as one with Welsh forebears, Liz rates Cardiff, where the Professional–Amateur Championships used to be held, very highly. 'It has been lucky for us, and what a place for a show, right in the centre of a city. Two minutes from the stables to the best shops . . . if there's time I never miss the shops during shows.' However, sadly Cardiff is no longer a part of the show circuit.

The facilities were both extensive and excellent, the ring level and not too big, with the stables set back in a large grassy area with plenty of room to work the horses. The singing from a group of Welsh cob and pony breeders down from the mountains to give a display, strongly supported by Sir Harry Llewellyn, owner of the immortal Foxhunter, and who always took a special interest in this show, and Harvey Smith, provided a superb end to one late-night party at the Angel Hotel over the road from the castle.

Very often Cardiff clashed with Aachen, deservedly the Mecca of the continental shows. Without a horse of scope it is wiser not to make the trip, for the courses in this superb, permanent, perfectly maintained arena, which also boasts permanent stands, are among the world's most demanding and victories are both hard sought and hard fought.

Aachen, an elegant town that was once the seat of the Emperor Charlemagne, is only just over the Belgian–German border and an easy journey from Warwickshire, taking only a day in the horse-box.

The conditions for the horses, stables and working areas are unquestionably the best. The only criticism is that while the horses have to give their all to win, the prize money has not been increased, even to keep up with inflation.

There is always a full entertainment programme including an evening party at the Club Zero in the International Spielcasino. The British team stays at a hotel near the ground and every night team manager Ronnie Massarella takes all his riders into the centre of town to an excellent Italian restaurant helping to keep British morale high in this shrine of show-jumping.

In 1981 Liz paid her first visit to the Paris CSIO, which is held at Longchamp, and she found it a really enjoyable experience. This show is held in the centre of the racecourse and is very compact with the stables, parked lorries and collecting ring all together. There is also all the room in the world to exercise the horses. Everything is portable and the permanent stands are not utilised. As is to be expected in July, the weather in Paris was perfect with the stables, collecting ring and the jumps living up to their reputation of being big but good. Liz describes them as being 'jumpers' courses, just the type you hope for when you are fortunate enough to ride as good a horse as Everest Forever'.

The hotel here is 'just a place to have a bath and lay your head down', because the show provides first-class food throughout in marquees on the ground.

The Royal Agricultural Show which is held on the first Monday to Thursday of July at Stoneleigh attracted a crowd of almost 200,000 in 1982 and, as always, the approach roads were clogged

Royal Horse Show, 1983. Four people worrying about a problem that was not theirs. From left to right: Derek Ricketts, Nick, Liz and the author. (*Bob Langrish*)

with cars and lorries throughout.

For the Everest Stud it may be the number one agricultural show but it is also very much their local show as it is virtually on their doorstep, being just down the road. This is a great energy saver as the horses can go back for a proper rest in their own stables each night whilst saving some hefty showground box rentals.

At the Royal there are not too many competitors and the prize money is good. Liz says,

The Royal has been a happy show for us because we've often won there and lots of people we know locally, even those who are nothing to do with the horses, shout and wave to us and come and talk. If we are lucky enough to go well, they are so pleased.

One night during the show, Ted and Liz usually give a party for their show-jumping friends. In 1981, when they held their last one before moving to Rio Grande, sixty people enjoyed a barbecue at Ponderosa, held in the glasshouse because the house was too small and the weather so unreliable.

Sometimes Liz's brother David stays. It all depends on whether the sun is shining or thunderclouds looming over David and Ted's longstanding on/off feud.

Most show-jumpers rate highly the Great Yorkshire with its huge, beautifully laid-out arena and good fences, but Liz does not go every year because, generalising, she gets far more pleasure from driving south than north to shows as, 'the weather is likely to be warmer and I prefer the softer country'.

Enjoying an improvised shower, Ted on a baking hot summer day at the Kent County Show, 1983.

The three-day Kent County Show at Maidstone at the end of the same week is always a must for one of Ted's riders. It is one of Ted's favourite trips as it is so well run and all concerned, whether officials or gatesmen, are so welcoming and the atmosphere lighthearted. 'It doesn't matter who jumps there', explains Liz, 'we always have to go for Ted's sake.'

The Royal International Horse Show returned to the White City from Wembley in 1983 after a lapse of sixteen years. Many people feel as Liz does, 'The old White City remains something of a blur in the past.' She recalls watching Pat Smythe winning the John Player competition on Scorchin' right at the end of her career, Harvey taking seven classes at one show and all the wet shirts she had to dry after storms.

Although the Royal International was virtually lost the two

years when it was held in the huge Wembley Football Stadium, 1968 and 1969, the latter occasion was memorable for Ted because he won the King George V Gold Cup there on Uncle Max.

Everyone complained bitterly when the show moved indoors to the Wembley Arena, but Liz admits to liking it inside, 'At least we weren't out in the bad weather we so often get for one or two days in the third week of July. And, once you went through the curtains into the arena, you were guaranteed perfect going, which means so much.' Ground conditions have varied from being holey to hard, and even puddingy, but those problems have been ironed out. There was also an invaluable covered marquee for the horses to work in, introduced after the disastrous rain of 1981 which reduced conditions to a quagmire.

During the Royal International Horse Show and Horse of the Year Show Liz and Ted stay in the adjacent Eurocrest Hotel. Although it cannot help showing signs of the million and one football supporters who have kicked their way through its doors, the hotel offers comfortable beds, baths and an above-average, especially for a north London suburb, midnight dinner menu; the accommodation is infinitely more restful than six nights in the horsebox. As there is no Nations' Cup and therefore no British team, a visit to this show is entirely at Ted and Liz's personal expense.

Normally the Hickstead International follows the week after the Royal International, although in 1983 it was held in May because of the European Championships. If a rider is a British Team member at Hickstead, he is then entitled to stay free at nearby Stroods Motel.

Astute Douglas Bunn, the 'Master of Hickstead', looks after his friends very well. They include most of the world's leading riders, bar those who have blotted their copybooks for a variety of reasons. So, if not in the team, Dougie will offer to accommodate a small ultra-select band of riders, sometimes including Ted and Liz. Liz explains,

> Most times, courtesy of Mr Douglas Bunn, we have one of his little flats. He also has two bungalows and other accommodation, and anyone who is staying anywhere as his guest is automatically invited into his house, Hickstead Place, to eat. He really is a number one host.

For all of the British riders, the Nations' Cup at Hickstead is the one where they hope to excel and jump two clear rounds. Says Liz,

> I get the most satisfaction from winning a Nations' Cup in England, my own country. I consider it a privilege to be selected for Britain at home because all the riders are available. Other than Calgary, where the financial rewards are high, there are very few other shows where the same holds good, by which I mean everyone hopes like mad to be selected.

After the third meeting at Hickstead at the beginning of August, the major events become rather thin on the ground except for the riders going on to the Royal Dublin Show at Ballsbridge. This is a show which anyone remotely interested in horses could not fail to enjoy because there is so much going on both in and around the white-railed paddocks that there is no chance to get bored. Just about every horse is for sale, most at astronomical figures, and the art of the blarney is demonstrated to the hilt.

Although the Irish are more interested in hunting than show-jumping, the main-ring stands are always packed on Friday afternoon to watch the Nations' Cup for the Aga Khan Trophy. It is preceded by the stirring drums and saffron-kilted swirl of the band which brings national fervour to a pitch. Riders such as Paul Darragh, Gerry Mullins and Eddie Macken are at their most dangerous on this afternoon, even without horses of the calibre of the late Boomerang.

At the end of August Liz frequently chooses a trip to St Gallen in Switzerland and Donaueschingen over the German border as an alternative to the Hickstead Derby. They are run with all the efficiency expected at an international show but without massive Aachen-type fences. 'St Gallen is a very gay town,' Liz asserts. 'Last time I was there, a festival was being held rather like the Mardi Gras, with competitions and dancing, bands and fancy-dress parades ... the whole town seemed to be in the streets.'

The jackpot of all the foreign shows is Calgary which is held in early September and Liz clarifies,

> It's the meeting to which everyone wants to go. It is run by Ron Southern and expense is no object. We have the best of every-

thing and the stabling is second to none. We stay at the Four Seasons Hotel in Calgary, which is first class, at the show's expense. It is situated some twenty minutes' drive from the Spruce Meadows showground and is set amid marvellous scenery.

The date of the Calgary show was chosen in the hope it would coincide with the Albertan Indian Summer but one time Liz was there,

> They sure missed it. There were unbelievable storms. One morning I woke up to find everywhere was white with snow. We just hoped for more snow by lunchtime so the day's classes would be cancelled, or for the sun to melt it. We managed to jump every day but it was desperately cold.
>
> We thoroughly enjoy the Canadian way of life, which is completely relaxed and casual. All I need to take to Calgary is two pairs of jeans, rough ones for the daytime and a best pair to wear at night. We visit different people's houses for barbecues, go up into The Rockies and maybe visit the famous hot sulphur springs at Banff. The country's clean, the hospitality great and so is the money.

The 1983 Grand Prix carried a first prize of £20,000, at the time a world-record high.

Back home, the one-day Camberley Show, which takes place on the lawns in front of the Royal Military Academy of Sandhurst, is one of the last of the good one-day outdoor shows. As it is put on by the Army, it is extremely efficiently run and as the going is usually perfect, Liz rates it a show to which it is worth taking a good horse.

Once autumn comes around, Liz finds that people make a lot of fuss about starting to jump indoors, but, she believes, 'a good horse will make the change without even bothering'. The Edgars usually hire the Balsall Common Arena to give the horses a jump inside before their first indoor fixture, The Everest Double Glazing Show.

Owner Bob Old always makes a wonderful effort when the three-day Everest Double Glazing Show is staged at his Park Farm

Arena, at Northwood, North London, at the end of September, the week before the Horse of the Year Show. 'The hospitality is endless,' says Liz, 'and we usually stay in the local hotel, thanks to Everest Double Glazing.'

The Everest Show aims to cater for every standard of horse from Foxhunter to International and to provide the ideal introduction to the indoor season. It also gives the juniors and young riders a chance to get some useful practice before Wembley some four days later.

It goes without saying that the Everest riders are especially keen to excel at their sponsor's own show, but despite their special endeavours, an Everest rider on an Everest horse has by the end of 1983 only once won the Championship. That success came in 1972 when Ted won on Snaffles when the show used to be held at the National Equestrian Centre.

The Horse of the Year Show at Wembley the following week with its electric atmosphere is most English enthusiasts' favourite show. There is also a sense of sadness, as people who have competed against each other week in, week out for six months up and down the country, make their farewells for the winter.

But, from at least one rider's angle, the show is not the greatest. Liz does not enjoy it as much as the Royal International:

There are more people there which makes for more pressure. Also we start at the ungodly hour of nine in the morning. To give the organisers credit, they have tried to make it later and now the only really early start is the Foxhunter on Tuesday, and perhaps Saturday. I find it a very tiring show.

The problem is that we jump so late at night – sometimes till eleven – and it makes a big difference if we don't have to start until eleven the next morning. The situation is not so bad at the Royal International because there are not so many competitors or classes.

There is no way I want to eat much in the day if I've got to ride my horse at night – I think you go a little better if you are a bit hungry. After the last class you definitely want a meal, but however you plan it, you cannot manage to be changed and sitting at a dining table before 11.30 p.m. at the earliest. It's totally the wrong time to eat but you do so because you are hungry. More often than not, we eat at the hotel because they put on a special service, a late night carvery, and serve us well. The show is exhausting because of the continuing late nights, early mornings and always having to push through that mass of people.

The Stoneleigh Autumn Championships at the National Equestrian Centre, usually held the week after Wembley, are low key, well run and enjoyable, an ideal place to take young horses.

The winter season which lasts from October to March takes place on two levels: at small local shows, which are mainly used to bring on novices; and at World Cup Qualifiers whose target is a place in the final the following April.

The first World Cup Qualifier is usually Amsterdam, one of the oldest shows. Liz first visited it in 1960 when it began and the show was held in the Heineken Brewery. It was her first venture over the water. The show is run by Ben Arts who has become a good friend to Liz over the years. The only criticism of this enjoyable show is the money: 'It's only worthwhile the last day; we jump for peanuts the first few days.' The present venue is an enormous complex where everything is under one roof.

Liz believes the Dublin Indoor Show, held at Simmonscourt over the road from Ballsbridge, is

not as well supported as it should be. The Irish make every effort to get things right for us. You can be sure of a laugh and that the courses won't kill your horses. Sometimes there are classes for ponies and Marie comes too.

It is a long drive through East Germany to the Berlin International and the oval arena where the show is held is some distance out of town. When Liz went with Everest Wallaby, the late Caroline Bradley was also competing. Early each morning they left the hotel in the town to exercise the horses. They walked together down the street and caught the local train, notable for its hard, wooden, uncushioned seats, which was the cheapest and easiest way of getting out to the stables.

Nick is the only Everest rider to have competed at Bordeaux and rates the long journey well worthwhile. 'We are wined and dined

to a very high standard.' The arena, which is by a lake, is part of
the Foire Internationale de Bordeaux Complex, and within easy
walking distance of the hotel.

Two weeks before Christmas, the riders are in Paris, which is
sparkling with lights and decorations. The show is held at a massive
complex similar to the National Exhibition Centre with a number
of halls. The lorries are parked just outside which is very con-
venient.

Liz went in 1981 and found the ground a bit sandy and holding:

> The horses were making dreadful mistakes. I had Forever in a
> class the first day and although he was clear in the first rounds
> and the jump-off, he got stuck twice and hit one fence very hard.
> After that I didn't jump him again till the Grand Prix on the last
> day. I just sat, waiting for the organisers to get the ground right.
>
>   Forever jumped three clears in the Grand Prix and finished
> second to Switzerland's Willi Melliger on his bay Trumpf Burr.
> I had the pleasure of putting Nick and St James into third place
> and Nick joked, 'It serves you right getting beaten because
> you've beaten me.'

In Paris the riders are put up in the Sofitel, which is excellent and
a reasonable walk from the show – 'We always walk because the
traffic is so bad.' Usually the riders only jump in the evening and
as Liz is fortunate in that Forever doesn't need much work, she is
able to visit the shops, only ten minutes away.

On the subject of the Olympia Christmas Show, Liz feels that,
'Unless you have decided to do the World Cup Qualifiers, I don't
think there's much point in going. It means a special effort, getting
a horse up and fit and interrupting his winter rest.'

Liz has competed in earnest there several times since 1977 with
Wallaby and Makedo and also Forever, although he has not
produced his top form in the elegant Victorian hall. Makedo was
well suited to the arena, and won a number of classes. Liz clearly
remembers winning the Radio Rentals Christmas Cracker Stakes
on Mayday, in 1975:

> It was one of my most exciting wins ever, and exciting is the
> word for it comes very near to fear. It was a feat on its own to

have behind Mayday horses of much higher calibre – François Mathy on his Montreal Olympic bronze-medal horse, Gay Luron, was second and David's Sportsman third.

Mayday was a horse I could never control that well, so I always made a plan beforehand of exactly where I was going to go, how I would place him and exactly how many strides I would take between fences because I couldn't alter him. With most horses you can change your mind and put in six strides instead of five, but with this horse, oh no. That day my plan actually worked. The last two fences were a parallel and a wall with a distance of nineteen yards, definitely four strides. I decided on a short angle and did it in three, Mayday cleared the 5 feet 4 inch wall, leaping out of stride.

No one else attempted three strides. If my plan hadn't come off, it would have been curtains at the wall. When the horse's feet leave the floor in such a situation I offer a little prayer and when I reach the other side, I say thank-you.

Marie has competed in the 12.2 h.h. classes at Olympia and has twice been second, once to Lee Johnsey, younger brother of Montreal Olympic rider Debbie Johnsey. Whether she is competing or not, Marie comes up for only a couple of days as Liz thinks the whole show is too much for any child. Marie usually persuades Liz's mother to go shopping with her and together they exhaust the London stores. 'When I tell my mother she shouldn't spoil her, she replies, "That's what nannies are for," and that's the answer to that.'

Then it's home, and flat out, hell for leather, for Christmas. I try to get all my parcels before Olympia but I'm afraid I seldom do. While I'm there I go out shopping in London in the mornings and make my yearly trip to Harrods, buying last-minute presents. When I get home I have to wrap them all up and worry about who I've missed.

It's a desperate rush and I get back to a terrific lot of hard work getting the meal together and preparing everything ready for Christmas Day. When it comes it's a terrific relief.

The Edgars always spend Christmas Day at home. The horses are done first, then the family has breakfast and opens all the presents which Marie has put under the tree. 'People call in and have a few drinks. We gorge ourselves at lunchtime on turkey, watch the telly in the afternoon, sitting bloated in our chairs and stay at home in the evening.' It is one of the rare days when Ted, Liz and Marie relax together all day long at home.

CHAPTER ELEVEN

1983 AND THE FUTURE

In February 1983, Lesley, hopeful of being selected to ride in the Los Angeles Olympics, said she wanted to ride for Ted and Liz 'for as long as they will have me'. Ted, whilst no advocate of the Games (he considers the huge courses which featured at the three recent full Olympiads in 1968, 1972 and 1976 were far too demanding of the horses), had singled out the Countess of Inchcape's Whato as her likely partner.

By the time the Royal Windsor Horse Show was held in May Lesley had left the Everest Stud in a furore of publicity, moving to a new base with Birmingham boxing promoter Pat Lynch at Balsall Common, Warwickshire. With Ted's full agreement, she took two horses with her: Cliff Cox's mare FMS Barbarella, formerly a regular winner for Nick, and the less-experienced Barbarossa.

The whole concept of sport in general, and certainly what it takes to win and keep doing so in show-jumping, has totally changed. Its former Corinthian atmosphere fell victim to fast-changing standards soon after the last war as sponsorship made a hesitant start and gradually gained momentum. Now, whether amateur or professional, the vital ingredient of winning remains natural talent. In addition, total dedication and determination, allied with endless hard work to achieve and maintain the high standard necessary for success, are essential. Early mornings, late nights, never-ending schooling and practice are common. Incessant travel – spending night after night in the horse-box or in ubiquitous faceless hotel-rooms where restaurants and room service have often closed long before the last competition ends – is all part of the scene.

The immense self-discipline necessary to reach top-class show-jumping is magnified when success comes as quickly as it did for

Lesley. Hers is an undeniable talent, but few would disagree that if she had not had the advantage of Ted and Liz as her mentors and their help in schooling her horses and in providing an endless flow of mounts – such as One More Time who was bought specially for her to win the European Junior Show Jumping Championship – she would not have come so far so fast.

But with success, stress and strain rapidly escalate and the world's best riders acknowledge that the problem of staying at the top is harder than getting there; but with their experience they have the advantage of knowing that the work will not diminish.

Recently, a US teenage tennis star who was virtually unbeaten gave up the sport because she could not cope with the demands her prowess had imposed upon her. For a teenager, this means a very reduced social life and it can be frustrating watching contemporaries doing the rounds of discothèques and parties. It is all a question of self-motivation, aims and personal choice: something about which the great Caroline Bradley – one of the world's best lady riders ever and a good friend of Liz's – had no doubts.

By the beginning of September 1983, Lesley had her first senior British team trip to Bratislava, Czechoslovakia, behind her and two Nations' Cup clears at Liège, Belgium, to her credit. Lesley had taken her decision to go ahead and do it her way, on her own. She is undoubtedly outstanding among her generation.

Even at the relatively tender age of thirteen years, Marie Edgar is a realist, like her parents. This approach to life bodes well for the future of the Everest Stud in which, eventually, she seems likely to be involved. When asked which were her favourite books, she replied, 'Oh, Diana Pullein-Thompson's. There is only one thing wrong with them, though, they all have happy endings and it's not always like that with horses and ponies.' And in 1983 the Everest Stud had its share of ups and downs in its horses' fortunes.

Although Ted had travelled some thousands of miles to buy Grand Prix horses for Liz and Nick, he could not find on offer at a feasible price, the type of jumper he wanted for Nick. Nick's hand was strengthened when Terry Clemence sent St James back to Rio Grande, ostensibly for the 1983 season.

Forever seemed to have benefited enormously from the winter rest and gave cause for celebration with three important wins in

March (Antwerp), April (Birmingham) and the season's first Hickstead meeting (May Bank Holiday), in peerless style, routing top-class opposition with Liz serene, accurate and in total command.

At the Royal Windsor Horse Show, Nick won the Modern Alarms Classic Grand Prix with St James. Both he and Liz were on the six-strong short list for the European Championship at Hickstead in July with an optimistic chance of making the final four for the team.

But that was not to be: Forever dispelled his chance with a disappointing round in the very deep going at Hickstead at the Everest Double Glazing Nations' Cup Meeting at the end of May. He pulled up fractionally lame and was withdrawn before the second round.

'There is,' Liz considers, 'one disadvantage in having a really outstanding horse: people are so used to him going well that it is barely noticed, then one below-standard round sets everyone talking.'

Forever was soon back in winning form, taking the Everest Double Glazing Class at the Three Counties Show at Malvern, two weeks later. Then, subsequently, although Liz was a member of the British team in Paris in June, she was not chosen to ride in the Nations' Cup competition there, despite the fact that the going was firm – ground conditions on which Forever produces his best form.

Denying Forever a chance of redeeming his Hickstead team performance, the Selectors plumped for Malcolm Pyrah, Nick Skelton, Harvey Smith and David Broome for the European Championship at Hickstead at the end of July.

Disaster struck in the appalling going that ruined most of the jumping classes at the Royal International Horse Show's return to the White City in July, when St James fell early on in the week, ripping open the outer side of a knee, mercifully missing the main artery and ligaments by a hair's breadth.

Immediately, Ted set off north with Marie and St James for Ratley, north of Banbury, in Warwickshire. It was close on midnight when he arrived to find John Williams – who is responsible for the Everest Stud horses' veterinary care at home – and the practice senior, Peter Thorne, waiting at red alert in the operating theatre.

The injury was cleaned, stitched up and thick strapping put on to immobilise the knee and hasten recovery. Nick was out of the team and replaced by John Whitaker who went on to take the individual silver medal on Ryan's Son. David Broome's intended partner, Last Resort, went lame and was replaced at Hickstead by his second string, Mr Ross. The British team finished second to Switzerland. St James did not compete again until September at Munich. At the end of the month he carried Nick to his first Everest Double Glazing Championship.

In blazing July heat, Forever did not excel in the waterlogged White City arena where the watering system had been left on too long through negligence. Otherwise, he resumed his winning ways, collecting the Lincolnshire, Hampshire and Kent County AITs.

Liz's disappointment over her non-selection for the European Championship, when it became a virtual certainty the going would be good to firm, was nothing compared to the hurt of being left out of the British team for Rotterdam in mid-August. The Selectors' somewhat vengeful reasoning was that she had asked not to be considered for the substitute Olympics in 1980: this did not assuage her feelings.

In 1980, Forever had been below par, following the effects of a blood disorder, and the going in the permanent arena at Rotterdam seemed likely to be heavy and, thus, not in Forever's favour. But in the wonderful record summer of 1983, which the weather experts correctly forecast would continue, she was surprised to be yet again discarded.

But survival is the name of the game, so Liz made alternative plans and in late August set off with Nick to the South German circuit, winning three Grand Prix at Eicherloh, Donaueschingen and Munich, with Forever. At Donaueschingen she was chosen to act as chef d'équipe for the Young Riders' Team, who were also competing there.

Nick's 1983 season was punctuated with horse problems. If Ever won the Gothenburg Grand Prix and was then laid up in the latter part of the summer with an over-reach. Halo, now owned by the Earl of Inchcape, sustained a minor injury during the summer, which put him out of action until the 1983–4 winter.

Domino, two years younger, is also owned by the Earl of Inchcape; he is now ridden by Nick and shows all the promise which can be expected from a horse of his age and experience.

That grand old stager, Maybe, was still winning classes such as a £1,000 first prize at Harlow; but his advancing years, coupled with the effects of the superb effort he made for Britain in the 1980 Substitute Olympics, mean he must now be considered a national horse.

Looking ahead, the nine-year-old Radius is Nick's immediate star hope. In 1983 he was not unduly pushed, but won useful classes, including one at Kent County, and he scored his first international success at Dinard. He has all the credentials to become a consistent international horse, just needing a few good breaks.

In June 1983, Ted was able to buy the German-bred mare Arabesque for Liz from Astrid, Venezuelan-born wife of German Olympic gold medallist Hans Winkler. The attractive Arabesque has an occasional soul-destroying stop, but once this problem is resolved, Liz may well have a second Grand Prix horse. She hopes to jump Arabesque in the 1983–4 World Cup Qualifiers.

Ted flew to Ireland in August 1983, the day before the Royal Dublin Horse Show opened, and bought for Liz an Irish-bred horse, Golden Privet, who was sold by the partnership of Belgian rider Alain Storme and Paul Darragh. A flaxen-maned and -tailed chestnut, he did not jump at Ballsbridge and Liz has found him to be 100 per cent honest with lightning reactions: 'He learns fast and is a quick jumper; a bit "spooky", like St James.' Liz thinks that spooky horses are often careful, and she plans to bring him on in the winter of 1983/4 with his first target the Grades C and B Championship at the 1984 Royal International.

As the horses at Rio Grande must change, so too, to a degree, must the support members of the Everest team. Nanny Julie left as planned in mid-summer 1983, to train as a nurse, and her place was taken by Pat Mitchell.

'Hob' (Fenella Power, daughter of former South Staffordshire MFH Michael Power) came to Liz as a teenager and stayed nine years, progressing from groom to a position of considerable authority before leaving after the 1982 Royal Show. She now lives with her father, near Rugeley in Staffordshire, but still comes back to do various jobs, such as fetching Arabesque from Germany. Liz evaluated, 'Hob is so natural with horses; because of her marvel-

ABOVE Arabseque – 'She's beautiful and she's mine,' says Liz. (*Bob Langrish*)

OPPOSITE: Arabesque and Liz heading for the tent for a practice jump at the Horse of the Year Show at Wembley, 1983. (*Bob Langrish*)

lous placid nature, they quickly trust her. She was just the person to give confidence to Makedo, who was very nervous and a wind-sucker, when we bought him.'

Seventeen-year-old newcomer Pip Lyons, who came to Rio Grande soon after Lesley left, is a first-class worker for whom nothing is too much trouble. 'He can stay with us for as long as he likes,' said Ted, after Pip had been with him for three months. Pip, whose family lives in Staffordshire, is gradually getting more competition confidence and, last summer, won a £100 Young Riders' Final at the Gate Inn Show from some stiff opposition, on Flame.

Ted has placed Lesley's former mount, the Countess of Inchcape's Whato, with Tony Newbery, with the thought in mind that they might form a partnership worthy of serious consideration for

the Los Angeles Olympic Games. Whato has the scope – the problem is his 'buzzy' mind. It is probable that Ted will ask Tony to ride other horses for him.

For Nick, the essence is winning. He possesses all the credentials, plus the desire and aggression to continue in this vein. When he married Sarah Edwards in October 1982, after a three-year on/off courtship, he chose an attractive wife well-equipped to support him and understand the foibles of the close world of show-jumping; simultaneously, Sarah became a respected fringe member of the Everest entourage.

Sarah, who reckons she could ride before she could walk, is an amazingly hard worker and has a close-knit and solid family background. Her father, Charles, breeds horses and seldom has less than fifty at his home in Duddleston Heath, Shropshire. Sarah's mother, Sue, met her father jumping horses in London and put in some of the early work on such well-known horses as Severn Valley and Severn Hills. Sarah's nineteen-year-old brother, Carl, represented Britain in a Young Riders' team in 1983.

Nick and Sarah live at Oak Cottage, Beausale. During the first year of their marriage, Sarah completely transformed the formerly run-down sixteenth-century timbered cottage. It gleams throughout and she has put the skills taught her by her grandmother to good use, making all the curtains and bed covers with an expert hand.

Outside, there are five boxes, housing her own Sherwood who has proved a first-class servant and carried her into third place in the 1982 BSJA Ladies' Championship, novice jumpers owned by Mr Harold Rose and Mr and Mrs Mike Phillips, and the latest of the series of the young horses she breaks and makes.

Liz does not plan to retire from show-jumping yet but adds, 'I shall quietly phase myself out over the years and remain involved even then. I plan to continue in international competition, while Forever is going well. He will be my guide line. When he retires, I probably won't enter for so many major classes. Marie reckons she is going to pinch him anyway for the Young Riders' Competition when she is old enough. If, in a year or two's time, I am lucky enough to have another top-class young horse, I might well want to ride him in international classes.'

Despite his occasional blustering and oft-bluff exterior, it must be recorded that Ted can also be extremely sympathetic. Sarah is among those who have found him more than ready to help with advice about any problem she has with her youngsters. Dressage rider Jane Kidd recalls being worried she would have to jump a big fence for Ted when he came to see a horse she had for sale and she had recently hurt her back. 'Just pop over a low pole, that's all I need to see,' Ted reassured her when he realised the problem.

Liz remembers, 'Just before Marie was born Ted had a rather special offer for Timmie which he would have liked to accept, but he turned it down because I was used to riding the horse. Quite rightly, he thought I might not be keen on competing, if I had to start again on a strange horse.'

The riders that Liz expects to see in continuing opposition to Nick include the Whitaker brothers, John and Michael: 'They did not come up quickly, are fighters and will endure.'

The future of show-jumping, as well as that of the participants, is of concern to Liz. Television viewing figures are certainly down on the boom days of the mid-seventies for annually televised events such as the Royal International and Horse of the Year Shows, but not desperately so in relation to most other sports. Also, the effect of video must be borne in mind.

However, the 1983 European Show Jumping Championships, which were held at Hickstead, produced excellent statistics showing there is still great interest in a special event. The BBC's figures for the last two days of the four-day meeting were;

Saturday 30th July	'Grandstand'	2.4 million
Sunday 31st July	'Sunday Grandstand'	3.7 million
Sunday 31st July	22.00 – 23.30 hrs	1.5 million

By no means all, but some TV commentary has been ill-informed and the fact that mistakes were made in some results in 1983 cannot help. The now retired Dorian Williams, whose fine speaking voice and enviable vocabulary originally helped attract viewers, could imply a sense of occasion in a unique and irreplaceable manner.

The lack of identity of horses brought about by absurd sponsored names and also the same name being handed on to another horse have, undoubtedly, contributed to the loss of interest.

Meanwhile, official statistics reveal that prize money continues to increase. The figures for England, Scotland and Wales are:

1948	£49,000
1966	£161,833
1975	£416,771
1982	£1,344,173

In 1983, the total was likely to be approximately £1,500,000. Inevitably, the expenses of competing continue to escalate, but it is noticeable that there are more and more expensive lorries – £40,000-plus jobs – on the circuit.

Overall, the crowds have lost their initial enthusiasm and there are not now so many spectators, except on big occasions such as the Hickstead Derby. They are tired of seeing the same jump-off formula, night after night. One reason they enjoy the Puissance is because it is different. New ideas are needed, but evolving them is more easily said than done.

Liz regards Dougie Bunn as 'A show-jumping visionary. Not so long ago, he told me his dream was to put on a two-day experimental show. There would be warm-up classes on the first day, and a £20,000 first prize Grand Prix on the second day.'

The days of struggle, of wondering where to find the next £100 are, thankfully, cast behind the Edgars; but even so, quite typically, Ted set up a business to help alleviate his financial problems, buying horses through an Irish friend, bringing them over to England to school them and generally smarten them up, before sending them back to Ireland to be sold for an increased sum. However, even Ted gave a rueful chuckle, as he related that one such horse was inadvertently sold back to its former owner – who did not recognise it – for £1,000 more than when it had changed hands only a few months earlier!

However the sport develops, the Edgar/Everest alliance will remain in the news in the immediate future. Ted, a supreme tactician in both placing horses and ringcraft, will sustain his efforts to help his riders blend their physical and mental abilities to maximum advantage. Simultaneously, fully aware of the voracious need of the media for close contact, his colourful, larger-than-life style and certain panache will not diminish.

Nor will his search for jumpers. Ted will continue to fly, thousands of miles each year, to find the horses necessary to keep his riders in ascendance. As explained, he will not be picking the best-looking horses, but will bear the following old rhyme in mind:

THE SHOW-JUMPER

I'm any old breed on the top of the Earth,
    Any old shape or size,
But mostly my quarters are lengthy and full,
    Lengthy and full my size;
My manners are good as a general rule,
    But chiefest of all, I'm wise.

And whether I come from John O'Groats,
    Newcastle Town or Dover,
He makes me go canterty, canterty, canter,
    Lickity, click, and o-ver!

from *Hoofbeats* by Homer Hawkins

OVERLEAF 'Good-bye folks.' Ted, who has already bought horses from the States, Holland, Denmark, Belgium, France, Germany, Ireland and Sweden, leaves to see a prospect in Australia.